What people are saying about

Bog Witch

In this inspiring book you will find the beauty and mystery of nature. Mab Jones writes with passion and poetic sensitivity about these often forgotten landscapes that breathe and bubble with nature's abundance. Your heart will be touched by the call to care for these wonderful wetlands.
William Bloom, leading UK spiritual author and teacher

Mab Jones' *Bog Witch* is beautiful, thoughtful, and thought provoking. She conjures up an animistic way of seeing the natural world in a light that is akin to the older, reverentially mysterious world – a world that exists, still, for those with eyes to see, ears to hear, and a fertile imagination. Highly recommended.
Adele Nozedar, author of *The Hedgerow Handbook*

Bog Witch by Mab Jones is a book of truths, of exploration, of discovery, of reconnection, with ourselves, with Mother Nature, and with the planet! I am very glad I introduced the author to the wetlands of Cardiff.
Steve Andrews, author of *The Magic of Butterflies and Moths* and other Moon Books titles

Bog Witch

Mab Jones

Previous Books

Yubitsume (Indigo Dreams Publishing)
ISBN 978-1-912876-60-0

take your experience and peel it (Indigo Dreams Publishing)
ISBN 978-1910834206

111 Haiku for Lockdown (Infinity Books UK)
ISBN 979-8655855281

Bog Witch

A semi-mystical immersion into wild
wetland habitats: their myths,
magic, and meaning

Mab Jones

**MOON
BOOKS**

Winchester, UK
Washington, USA

CollectiveInk

First published by Moon Books, 2024
Moon Books is an imprint of Collective Ink Ltd.,
Unit 11, Shepperton House, 89 Shepperton Road, London, N1 3DF
office@collectiveinkbooks.com
www.collectiveinkbooks.com
www.moon-books.net

For distributor details and how to order please visit the 'Ordering' section on our website.

Text copyright: Mab Jones 2023

ISBN: 978 1 80341 187 3
978 1 80341 186 6 (ebook)
Library of Congress Control Number: 2023933658

A CIP catalogue record for this book is available from the British Library.

Design: Lapiz Digital Services

UK: Printed and bound by CPI Group (UK) Ltd, Croydon, CR0 4YY
Printed in North America by CPI GPS partners

We operate a distinctive and ethical publishing philosophy in all areas of our business, from our global network of authors to production and worldwide distribution.

Contents

I am not concerned that I have no place;
I am concerned how I may fit myself for one.
I am not concerned that I am not known;
I seek to be worthy to be known.

Confucius

Bog Witch

Double, double toil and trouble;
Fire burn and caldron bubble.
Fillet of a fenny snake,
In the caldron boil and bake;
Eye of newt and toe of frog,
Wool of bat and tongue of dog,
Adder's fork and blind-worm's sting,
Lizard's leg and howlet's wing,
For a charm of powerful trouble,
Like a hell-broth boil and bubble.
The three witches, *Macbeth*

Chapter 1

Toil and trouble

We walk. My friend says we must go past the science museum, to the roundabout, then left. I've not been to this part of the city before. Grey follows grey, and on one side of us is a road roaring with cars, buses, vans. The noise and motion are thick, disrupting all sense, exhaust smoke puffing up to join the drab cloud blocking out the sun above us...

I grew up in this city. The part of it I was raised in was, at that time, Europe's largest council house estate. My interactions with nature were few and far between, and restricted to things found in or on hedges as we walked the short route to school. This included ladybirds, caterpillars, and, once, a hedgehog. Although there was a stretch of grass opposite us, this was the sort of clipped green that was inhabited almost solely by dog walkers. On a few occasions, we walked or cycled further, because our estate was at the edge of the city: to go strawberry picking with our mum in hillside fields; or to the Drope where, past the posh houses, there was a river, and quite probably the plants and creatures associated with rivers, though I never noticed them at all.

My eyes, at that time, were blind to the beauties of nature. Life's toil was, in those working class environs, all around me. My mother worked hard to support her four children, working up to three jobs at one point. My father was a lazy, abusive bully. His special attentions, in a number of ways, focused on me. I was the eldest. And so, instead of escaping outwards into nature, where I'd already, at a very young age, experienced the potential of danger from men, I escaped into books, and into stories, mostly of space, the supernatural, and speculative realms; and, in my later teens, into the more mystical tales of Paolo Coelho, Carlos Castaneda, and Colin Wilson.

I was looking for magic – elsewhere. I'd no idea that magic was, in fact, staring me in the face, every time I looked out of the window at an ocean of green grass blades opposite.

We walk. The roundabout thrums with heavy goods vehicles; we stutter-breathe the thick, coiling fumes, before taking the left turn. Houses sit like rows of neat teeth on either side. It's a narrow road; the very edge of the city. We follow it down…

Life as a working class woman seemed designed to accustom me to toil. No-one in my family had ever finished school, let alone been to university. If I followed family tradition, I'd leave at sixteen and couple up before popping out the first in a line of kids. My mother had me at age eighteen; her mother, and her mother's mother, had started even younger. However, things were a bit different for me. I'd always loved reading, and my mother had encouraged me in this, when very young, by buying me books from a book club in school; and, later on, by taking me and my siblings on regular trips to the local library. Libraries are wonderful – gateways into the imagination. So, worlds, through words, were always there for me, and I have my mother to thank for that.

Ambition wasn't something that came easily however; it wasn't imbued in us; it wasn't innate. My parents came from abusive families themselves, and their parents did, too, so when I look back it's clear that if there was any tradition which we inherited, it was trauma. Working class people don't go to therapy, generally, and that certainly wasn't an option for my parents in the seventies and eighties. So, they just lived with it, and lumped it, and hoped they didn't become monsters themselves. Or, slowly realised that those sorts of monsters are something that always lurk within you. In any case, ambition was never a thing, but somehow, I was born with some of this; or maybe I was just a child of the ambitious eighties; or maybe I just looked at the long lines of women, my mother and her forebears, going back to whenever, who'd all been worn down by care, toil, endless housework and child rearing, and decided I didn't want to do the same. "What is it you plan to do / With your one wild and precious life?" asked the poet Mary Oliver. Well, not wash dishes and do laundry, I thought, even when still a child myself.

I was also born interested in spirituality. I wondered whether there was anything more to this life than the wholly physical world which was all around me. Working class people are, in my view, raised to become 'feeders and breeders' – to consume and birth future consumers; the whole set up, including education, is not to make you think, but to tell you what to think, and how to be. This is my own experiential viewpoint; perhaps you would argue differently. But, certainly, consumption was set up as a goal, as a primary ambition, as a 'joy', whether that was eating a thing or buying a thing or watching a thing on TV. To access these, we were required to give our time and energy to work. Needless to say, it would probably be work we hated, but that was the price and we were taught we should pay it.

Now, consumption threatens to destroy the entire Earth, of course. Already, in the eighties, songs like *Bigger, Better, Faster, More* were reflecting our greed back to us. We all know it's time to forget ambition and veer away from its insistence on a life of 'toil and trouble'. What point is there in becoming a mogul, or a millionaire, if you know that the empire you create will be swallowed by the sea in a century's time? It could be argued that people who aim to become incredibly rich don't care too deeply about other human beings to any great degree, because they will undoubtedly be reliant upon gaining their riches from workers and resources which will all be bought at the lowest possible cost. In our capitalist culture, cost, savings, and profit take precedence over concerns relating to human welfare or the environment. We choose the lure of money over the lushness of nature, again and again and again.

At the end of the slender street is a wall. It's as high as my head, so I cannot see beyond it. But, above, I observe the most beautiful, golden heads of feather grass, swaying in the wind. They look, to me, like magic. We turn right and follow the wall along, the grass blowing gently in our direction, like flags or hands, their elegant tendrils pointing out the way.

As a teenager in the nineties, there was a campaign to build a barrage down in the bay. I'd never been to the bay, but apparently the old wetlands there were a haven for birds and wildlife. It's a generalism, and individually it would be untrue, to say that working class people are not interested in birds and wildlife. But it wasn't instilled in us, and so we never went there. Our holidays were always linked to consumption – ice creams in the park, or renting a caravan on holiday. Enjoying entertainments, snacks and treats. We never went on a long walk or a hike; we never went camping; what would be the point of that? We weren't educated or raised to understand nature, and were cut off from it to a great degree.

So, I didn't really understand the argument that was being made at that time. I didn't know much about the campaign, and the city seeming so desolate to my tortured, teenage eyes, I honestly thought that shops and bars in the bay would be an improvement. Those in power thought so too, and campaigned hard for the change. A visitor centre shaped like a squashed toilet roll tube – intimating that wetlands are shit – was set up, and all the many advantages of the change were loudly proclaimed. The wetlands would be destroyed, and myriad birds would lose their homes – as would the local population of working class, mostly ethnically diverse people – but, think of the progress. Think of the profits!

The wall ends abruptly and I draw a small, involuntary breath. Beyond, are birds and water, grass and trees. It is beautiful. The feather grasses are gathered everywhere, tendrils swirling and unfurling, golden heads swaying in the breeze. There are rushes, looking to me like giant matchsticks, their bulbous heads darkly luminous against the blue and green. There is a jetty and, out on the water, there are coots and ducks, geese and goosanders, long-necked swans and great crested grebes, milling and swimming, serene on the cloud-reflecting water. My friend tells me these are the wetlands. I had no idea...

I had no idea, growing up, of the importance of nature. It's good for mental health, emotional health, and spiritual health. Over the course of the pandemic, many of us keenly felt the absence of a garden, and of being confined to man-made spaces alone. After learning of the wetlands – not the original site in the city; sadly the developers won out, and the wetlands described above were destroyed; these new wetlands were created a little further along from the bay in their stead – I moved to a house just opposite, and was lucky enough to be able to walk there most days.

If you visit the wetlands, you know that they are glorious, gorgeous places, filled with vibrant life. They buzz, hum, and sing. Animals within them swim, dip, and soar. Plants thrive, filching up from mud to dazzle and bloom. They are home to damselfly and dragonfly, newts and toads, otters and ospreys. Herons fly in on their silver wings to stand like priests at the mud-edge. Tadpoles form whole tides of riotous, wriggling life in the right season. There are plenty of resident birds and also rare bird visitors, who drop in for a day or two before heading off again. Beetles and bugs abound, as do, in this wetland kingdom near where I live, delicate flora such as bee orchids. It is wild, wonderful, and utterly enchanting.

Strange, then, that wetlands here are under constant threat from development. In only two years of being resident writer in the wetland next to my house, one not far away was threatened by a road development; another lost its protection by a local council due to cost. In Wales, there are many wetlands, because we have the coast on three sides. We keep trying to replace green with grey, however, and now have the added issue of coastal erosion to contend with. We assign the space around us a 'green value', a monetary equivalent, but not the value that's inherent within the green of grass, stem, and leaf.

I've come to learn that in order to change things, we must develop our 'green vision'. Saving nature mustn't be too much toil, it can't be too much trouble; we need to act now if we want to save our planet and, by extension, our own skins, and that change must happen on the inside – within us – beginning with how we view nature and our own place in it. We must first change ourselves if we wish to change – and save – the world.

Chapter 2

Fenny

Wetlands are an in-between place: not quite land; not quite water. As such, they're difficult to define; the edges of them may be indistinct; blurring; unclear. They also possess a wide variety of names. Fen, swamp, bog, billabong, delta, estuary, lagoon, peatland, mire, mudflat and marsh are some of them. Their presence in many countries and across international coastlines, or forming on the flood plains next to rivers, means that they may be named in a variety of tongues and dialects, and is yet another reason for the multiplicity of terms. There may be differences in these terrains, too, in terms of their composition, water type (freshwater, saltwater, or brackish water) and flora / fauna mix. But, generally, the term *wetlands* encompasses each of these, and each of the subtypes contains what we tend to associate with that wetland confluence of land and water – *mud*.

Mud, by rights, is dirty, stinky, and oozy. It is sticky, squelchy, unpalatable stuff. Wetlands are so-called because they are mud-filled. As a kid growing up in the eighties, two of my favourite films showed clearly what these natural places were like. One was the bog of eternal stench in *Labyrinth*; the other was the swamp of sadness in *The Neverending Story*. Both were muddy, mucky, grimy, grubby, grungy, gross. Both were deadly; dangerous. In those films, you got sucked into the silt-like mud and died, or were tainted by its pungent musk forever.

The only other references to these places that I knew of were *Boglins*, a type of ugly puppet toy favoured by my brother, and our toilet, which we all referred to as 'the bog'. It was the sort of place where I imagined Macbeth's witches might forage for their 'eye of newt', etc. There weren't any beautiful blooms there, for sure — nothing pretty or prize-winning. Just a lot of mud, and weird creatures and creepers caked in it. Hard to assign wetlands a 'green value' of the ecological sort, perhaps, when they are so consistently brown in hue.

Those three witches, in their famous incantation, use the word 'fenny' to describe one of their ingredients, which therefore we can assume originated in the fen. They are bog witches, potentially, then – drawing magical constituents from the swampish mire and, although many of the gruesome, ghoulish items they list – at least in the first part of their incantation, before they move on to utilising bits from baboons and sharks – were in fact quite possibly drawn from common folk names for plants and herbs, the images and animals are still those stemming from wetland habitats. This in and of itself demonstrates the richness of wetlands areas – they are full of flora which may be used in a herbal or healing capacity.

However, as a word, 'fenny' is similar to 'funny', and fens can, too, be comical. They're the dippy, drippy, lesser cousin of epic oceans, magical woodlands, wild moors, etc. They're more difficult to define, being made up of two intermingled elements with borders that are indistinguishable, and this makes them less dramatically appealing. As a poet, I can name plenty of poems taking the sea or the forest as their setting, but very few in homage to or even venturing into marshland. They are a bit too silly for very lofty verse. When you walk through fens, your boots often sink into their stool-coloured sludge, and when you pull them out there's a wet noise that's something like a fart. If you fall, of course, it isn't anything dramatic like in *The Neverending Story* or *Labyrinth* – you just get caked in filth, and your walking partner laughs at you. It's a nebulous place, and its creatures are more ugly-funny, perhaps, than those of other, more elemental territories: warty toads, weirdo newts, slowworms with their flat forked tongues and strangely lidded eyes.

Its cultural critters and creatures, also, are funny: bog monsters – hence the *Boglin* toy favoured by my brother – and 'swamp things', like the DC character of the same name. In Marvel comics, a creature called 'the Glob' is depicted as lumpy, near-featureless, and strung with slimy green plant tendrils and ooze. There are plenty of other marsh monsters of this sort in films, television, comics, and books, too, and their names are associative of lack of feature – 'thing' – and lumpishness – 'blob'. Further on in the swamp of sadness, the hero of *The Neverending Story* meets Morla, who is a kind of tortoise, it seems, except that her giant back looks rather more like a muddy clod than anything else. Soggy, blobby, clotty, and slow, the cultural creatures of the wetlands are hard to take very seriously.

From the silly, then, these entities veer towards the spooky and the sinister. This is particularly the case when we begin to look away from contemporary culture into the myths and legends that preempt them. Perhaps it's because we're now such a knowing, media-driven species, who can get a better grip on these muddy terrains through documentary and online articles, that we're able to laugh at our ancestors' fear of bog creatures by creating parodies in toys, tales, and images. Once, though, bogs were far more fearsome places, and that fear fed our imaginations and our resultant sense of them. The toy *Boglins* no doubt derive from mythical boggarts, and another word for them is 'boggle', which is the name of a character in childhood favourite *Labyrinth*. In English folklore, a boggart inhabits marshes and fens but can also be a malevolent spirit in the household. In Welsh, the boggart may be more readily linked to the pwca / bwga, or fairy folk, and is similarly mischievous in nature. Bogeymen are an associated entity, and it's clear, with that one, that the 'indistinct' aspect is far more terrifying than humorous.

Another forebear of the slimy green swamp thing is the river hag who – as in examples such as Peg Powler, a legendary hag of the River Tees in the Piercewood area of County Durham – often sports long green hair, as if made from the weeds of the tributary itself. Peg, like many other hags, is associated with a particular stretch of river, and delights in dragging the unsuspecting to their untimely demise deep in the watery abyss. Her counterparts in the UK include green skinned Jenny Greenteeth, who is familiar to those in the north-west of England; Grindylow Peg; Mary Hosies in the Avon in Lanarkshire; Nellie Longarms; and Jenny the Whinney on the Isle of Man. Cutty Drier in Dartmoor, Devon is a rare male counterpart of these women, who are all depicted as older, and unsightly. Here, the sense of 'fenny' lurches from 'funny ha ha' to 'funny peculiar' (before grabbing us by the wrist and dragging us mud-wards, of course).

These spirits are associated with water. Some patrol rivers; others lurk in ponds. Partly, it is thought, they were used as tall tales to keep the young and unwary from getting too close to the edge of dangerous watery spots and potentially falling in. What child wouldn't be afraid to venture out into the deep, dark wetlands, with their numerous pools disguised by reams of innocent-looking pondweed, if they knew that no-good Nellie was lying in wait for them? Interestingly, *Jenny Greenteeth* is also a name for pondweed (or duckweed), which often covers over, and therefore disguises, the presence of a wetland pool, pointing again to the cautionary nature of these spirits.

They serve a purpose, then – but, it is pertinent that these entities are mostly women, too, and older women in the majority of cases. The grey mud of wetland spaces is analogous to the grey skin of a very old white person, perhaps. Pondweed becomes her hair; ponds themselves are her watchful eyes, waiting for an unsuspecting person to venture too close, before transforming to a mouth, so she may swallow the poor interloper down (some of the hags above do, in their respective legends, also eat travellers). They are rough and raw, without affectation or even speech, and as such are more akin to working class women, perhaps; not ladies, princesses, or queens. At their best they are silly or stupid – "older women are objects of contempt and ridicule" – (Markson and Hess, 1980) – and at their worst they are malevolent – witches, in alliance with the devil, who gives them magical power in place of their wasting, waning looks.

In my eyes, as a working class woman, and a witchy one at that, I cast my own gaze upon that traditional one and I find it just as silly. There are no reasons other than sexism and ageism for casting old women in the role of hags and telling us they are evil. There is no reason other than ignorance and scapegoating to cast a whole habitat in the form of a crone and say 'she' is bad. An old woman in our society is a person of low value, with little cultural power. Her financial capability will be lesser – 23% of single female pensioners in the UK exist in poverty, compared to 18% of single male pensioners (Department for Work and Pensions, 2019). "The old suffer, not only from low incomes and poor health in comparison to younger people, but from a more pernicious deprivation-loss of function and status", and this is especially true of older women (Markson and Hess, 1980). She is invisible, very often; overlooked, ignored, as well as maligned. So it is with our wetland areas. Wetlands, too, exist on the margins, literally and also metaphorically; few people know of them, or of their value. Or, if they do know about them, then they are 'hags' in their imaginations – swampish mires, to be ignored and avoided at all costs.

Bogs are the opposite of picture postcard places. If they are reimagined as women, then they are the opposite of pin-ups. Hags are old, precisely because "the loss of perceived sexual attractiveness and reproductive function experienced by old women has been related to poor self-concept and how they are devalued by society at large" (Gibson, 1996). Again, the same goes for wetlands. Their spiritual symbol is the magical old crone; no wonder that Macbeth's three witches cite so many wetland plants and animals in their famous chant. They are inextricably linked. The trio's next verse goes on to cite 'shark…' and 'tiger…' but to an Elizabethan audience, at a time when the fens were being increasingly drained and devalued, the toady, warty, snaking creatures of a wetland habitat would have seemed just as strange and spectacular; just as vicious and evocative.

However, as a younger woman, I, too, feel an affinity with wetland habitats. I inhabit a body that I've often thought of as 'lumpish' – it is a body made for bearing children, and for nurturing them. It has seemed sludgy at times, with its fleshy deposits; its natural, womanly weight and fluctuations of fat. It's been mucky, with all the processes and proclivities of the female form, in particular the monthly mire of that most watery of workings: menstruation. That, in and of itself, has encouraged, in my thinking, an association of my own body as something gross; something always a bit icky and dirty. Like the wetlands, it has seemed festooned in filth, a curse I must always carry with me. At other times, it's been a joke, the object of sexist jibes and stereotypes. Certainly, these are thoughts that are, also, inherited, rather than innate, but they are reinforced by our culture, in which women's bodies, too, may be silly - boobies - or scary - cunt.

A comedian, up on a stage, if they are large or lumpish, unattractive or suffering from some other 'affliction' – say, being dark skinned, disabled, LGBTQ+, or female – will invariably begin their set by mocking this weak point in themselves, before the audience does it for them. In this way, they reverse that 'weakness', turning it into a source of power. The audience laughs, 'helpless'. They submit to the power of the comic. I've been that comedian, mocking my curves and femininity on a stage before crowds of drunken men and women got round to it first. This is one way of transmuting that image of the bog woman / bog witch, in my experience – you laugh at her / yourself, and the fenny woman (hag) becomes a funny woman instead.

However, this isn't, to me, either a healthy or a long-term solution. The issue lies in our reduction of women's bodies, and our notion of the earth's body, as objects, and of assigning them a value – these bodies / bits of earth have high value; these bodies / bits of earth have none. It doesn't help with self-acceptance when you are mocking your form on a stage, either. You are still objectifying 'it' – the body – through your ridicule. Loving your lumps is the only way to do it. As someone who hated her body, once, simply waking up and deciding to love 'it' isn't possible. It's been a long, slow process for me in which I have moved from hate to dislike; on, then, to acceptance; and even further, in recent years, to like and, sometimes, love.

It's easy to keep thinking of bogs, like bodies, as a joke. Damselflies gestate here as ugly bugs, fat larvae swimming in murk – but then they emerge like punchlines, like brilliant conclusions, for two weeks of life as an iridescent flying creature. Toads blink, beady-eyed, before their lolling bodies pop into the air like jumping beans and plop into the stool-coloured water. Flowers in this murk might be as bright and brief as firecrackers; there are many rare orchids in and near the wetlands next to my home, which are as strange and silly as the shapes they make – this one, which emulates a bee; this one, with a shape akin to a butterfly. They make brief appearances – for one week only! – demanding our attention, much like travelling clowns.

But a small shift in our thinking, and in our interpretation of what is before our eyes, transforms the bog from base to beautiful; from banal to breathtaking. The witch becomes *be*witching. We must learn to marvel at her boggy body, which gives life to moths and mushrooms, toads and tubers. Her processes are nothing short of miraculous. She may not be as pretty as a picture, but the picture she paints is perfect, and just as gorgeous in its own way. Like the female form, we must choose to see her strange, soggy body not as horrific, or as humorous, but as miraculous. We must peek into her pools and see not pollution, but wonder. Eventually, for me, those pools became a kind of mirror, reflecting my own image back to me, and telling me it was good. By transmuting the bog, we transmute the body, too. But, for the purposes of this short book, let's focus upon transforming our view of the wetlands, from swamp to splendour; from fen to fantastic. There's no need for the mind to boggle, or get bogged down, in this one. The magickal process of transformation is begun in the simplest of ways – we start by simply stepping out and into the wetlands themselves.

Chapter 3

Tongue of dog

I'm encouraging you to step into wetland spaces, even though as a child and young person I had no clue about their existence. Later, as a young person, I felt no strong need to explore there; my much stronger wish was to escape the city I grew up in. And so, I travelled to cities, further and further away; and then to countries, living for some years on the other side of the globe. Wales remained a murky, misty memory in my imagination. Wetlands weren't something I was consciously aware of although, thinking back, they were always bound up with my concept of what home was.

Additionally, when I was younger I had little experience of, and almost no appreciation for, nature. If I had a relationship to it, it was of nature as a 'thing' or 'object', for instance in the form of rare flowers we bought from the supermarket, say on Mother's Day, or in nature programmes on television, which we didn't really watch, although the TV in our tiny house was on for a minimum of twelve hours out of twenty-four, and often for longer than that. My mum had a few house plants, and we had a little bit of lawn in our back garden, but that was about it. There was a field opposite our house, as I've said, but I rarely went into it. When I looked over into the green expanse, I saw 'nothing' – nothing to do; nothing to entertain me, or to consume. Grass was not 'nature', to me. And nature itself, as well as being a thing, was also, somehow, an absence – a place free from civilisation. I didn't see the birds, bees, or bugs which no doubt teemed in that field. People took their dogs to walk there, and in that sense it was useful, but nothing more.

I would see these dog walkers over in the field daily. Conversely, I often feel that I was raised rather like a dog. One reason for feeling this is the way in which working class lives tend to run. We are bred to work: beyond this, we are encouraged to consume and to have children. As a child of the eighties, you might say that this is simply capitalism but, now that I know more people coming from middle class backgrounds, I have found that the consumption in these strata runs differently; as one example, my middle class partner grew up going for hikes and mountain walks; I did not. Nature was something one 'consumed', for us, rather than something we coexisted within. Being in nature for its own sake was not something we did, and not something we understood the point of. This is a class generalism, of course, but it is my experience.

Another reason for this 'dog' feeling comes from the sense of having been 'civilised'. Being cut off from nature, in a city, is one thing, but then there are the manners which one must learn and which are, to a great degree, embedded / enforced. We receive them in our upbringing and education; they are mirrored by our culture, and modelled by the adults around us. Aside from everyday civilities, which greatly ease and lubricate our relationships, and those habits and regimens linked to very good and useful things, for example, hygiene and cleanliness – which I'm sure we're all very glad of – a great number of manners, to me, seem to expand out from the need to lubricate our social interactions and enter into the arena of self-repression. 'If you can't say something nice, don't say it at all' is a maxim which ensures we don't cause offence to others. But what if we need to say that thing? What if the behaviour it relates to is damaging to us? Do we 'swallow it down'? Very often, we try to forget smaller offences; but what if they are larger? Should we not express our feelings, of anger or sadness, fear or distress, in that instance?

Much of the personal self-healing work I've done has been linked to unexpressed emotion. As mentioned, my father was abusive and, growing up, I often felt scared and under threat. If

I dared to bark my defiance, I was punished. I was not allowed to give voice to what I felt, and this caused the feelings linked to those potential expressions to remain within me; to sit, distill, and to then cause problems for me later on. Another saying is 'the truth will out', and for me it's this process of regurgitation and release that I had to go through in order to expel those held-in, pent-up feelings which, like splinters, had become festering and foul. I needed to extract them in order to heal. It was a long, lengthy, often laborious process. Much of it was magickal, but magic not as a fine, elegant, or rarefied thing – very often, it was dirty, messy, and painful, with physical, mental, and emotional repercussions and results. I repeatedly had to undertake challenging actions in the physical realm alongside this 'energy work' (meditation, reiki, spiritual healing, as three examples). Quite often, the greatest result, in the end, came from simply speaking what I had not spoken at the time, all those years ago. The greatest 'magic' and consequence, in the end, often came down to barking my defiance.

A dog was once a wolf, of course. A wild wolf symbolises freedom, but as a child and young person I never felt free. I felt trapped. It's fashionable now to talk and write about 'rewilding', but as well as planting flowers and trees, and cultivating our precious green spaces, how do we cultivate that innocent 'green-ness' of self? How do we regain the wild human part of ourselves who is, like the wild animals and wild flowers, at one with the earth and feels truly part of it? A wolf isn't 'civilised' as a dog is, but even a dog will howl. How do we reinvigorate ourselves with that same sense of freedom, that lack of submission; how do we regain the power to verbalise our emotions, and cry and shout freely, without fear or shame, now that we know it isn't wrong or bad to do so; and how do we retain that direct, defiant self-sense, which confidently puts aside the muzzle our culture has placed on us through its civilising, often suppressive, influence?

I think we can do this, in part, through nature. Poetry and people also played their roles in my journey, and energy work was paramount, but immersing into nature further assisted in this reconnection with self. I couldn't see the green of the field opposite my house, so for me the 'nature cure' was extreme – I went to live in Japan, and fell in love with the more tropical, and very colourful, beauty of Oriental gardens, mountains, and forests. These were very much a calming, healing balm to my tortured self. How tortured I was, I won't detail here, but it was enough for me to be able to say that I was a victim of childhood trauma, and to know that that dog-like sense came, also, from the cruelty dished out at the hands of my father. My purpose here isn't to detail the abuse, but this feeling of being an animal – a dog in my mind – persisted, from childhood into adulthood. I was a pet; closer to an object than a human being; a thing to be tamed, controlled, restrained, made to be obedient; a creature to be used, at will and against my own.

When I returned to Wales, I sadly couldn't take the gorgeousness of Japan with me. I had to learn to see the beauty of nature right here. Like that field, however, I found it hard to properly notice what I'd been brought up right next to. It's often overcast where I live, with spit-rain and drizzle a common occurrence. The greyness can sometimes be overwhelming. There are green fields, but they're not usually bursting with blooms or in possession of a riot of colour. Very often, in our lacklustre temperate zone, and sitting as we do on the gulf stream, the seasons seem to blur into each other, particularly in the city, with rainy greyness occurring at any time of the year and blurring earth into sky, pavement into rooftops. If, in some languages, there are multiple words for snow – our Celtic cousins who speak Scots possess 421 words for it, according to www.scotsthesaurus.org – then rain, here, is the equivalent. My cursory knowledge of our native Welsh throws up phrases without an English equivalent, such as 'sgrympian' – a short, sharp shower – and 'brasfrwrw' – big spaced out drops', as well as 'lluwchlaw' (sheets of rain), 'pistyllio' (fountain rain), and 'curlaw' (beating rain), amongst other phrases.

However, I had been woken up to the potential of beauty, and I knew that nature soothed me. It's healing capacity has been written about by many far more scientific minds than my own. It can reduce blood pressure and relieve mild depression; lessen stress and anxiety, anger and fear; and help us do away with repetitive or ruminating thoughts. In Japan, 'shinryuku', or forest bathing, is known to have a healing effect. In the west, 'ecotherapy' is currently on the rise, with interesting recent studies such as *Wetlands for Wellbeing* which proposes that "nature-based health interventions based in wetlands are an effective therapy option for individuals diagnosed with anxiety and/or depression" (Maund et al., 2019). The paper mentions the benefits of 'blue space' and 'green space' but 'brown space', it makes plain, also offers therapeutic benefits.

Gradually, I've come to terms with the greyness and browness of here. There is beauty, brilliance, and miracle set within it. Nowhere is greyer than a Welsh bog on a wet day, to my mind. Nowhere, hereabouts, is muddier, as the grey-brown muck mulches up, rising with the water level to become a sodden, soggy mire. It's marshy and it's gloomy. It's sludgy and it's sodden. If it is a female body, it is my body, as I've said; her voice, by this analogy, becomes my own.

When you walk into wetlands, it's the absence of sound that most profoundly marks the crossover from urban to wild. After the roar of the city, the first impression, here, is of silence: the absence of car engines and exhausts; of tyres on tarmac as drivers brake; of buses thundering and the growl of bikes; of building works and road works; and of all the chaos and cacophony of human beings, from their voices to their various machinations. In some Welsh wetlands, motorways and A-roads are never far away, and may still be audible; planes, until recently, were a regular interruption overhead; but, generally, these terrains take us away from the urban and set us down in the wild. Silence is typically what greets us first of all.

I, too, was a very quiet child – so quiet that I often didn't speak, sometimes at home, and sometimes at school. At the age of sixteen, I stopped speaking outside of the home, and often within it, withdrawing into myself. Later, both a therapist and a doctor stated that this sounded like selective mutism; but I think that, if it was, it was a mutism borne of trauma. Abuse took its toll on my self-esteem, and on my sense of self. Later, I came to poetry as another kind of balm, even though, initially, my poetry style was very performative, and all about satire and saying things that others deemed naughty or even offensive; around that age, in my late twenties, I was undergoing therapy, too, and it was appropriate that the 'unsayable' was articulated; that I allowed myself to speak as I wanted, and even to be cheeky and unchecked as I had never been allowed before.

Immersing into this aural absence, however, you realise, soon enough, that it isn't – there *is* sound here. However, it's unfamiliar; strange; even unsettling. In the city, we have sparrows and seagulls, pigeons and crows. There are starlings, song thrushes, pied wagtails, the various families of tit. We see robins regularly. We sometimes observe starlings as they group, gather, and go to their resting places. But here in the estuary exist a different set of birds. And so, instantly, this is a place that *is* different, with sounds and sonics that are markedly divergent.

An alternative dawn chorus exists here, an often off-kilter choir made up of the keening calls of coot and scratchy song of reed bunting, the hissing of squabbling swans and the mating calls of grebes as they swim-dance their mating ritual. The 'kip', 'kek' and 'kerr' of terns and "whinnies, cackles and yelps" of moorhens are common (the alternative dawn chorus, 2022). The famous curlew's cry, immortalised in the poem *He Reproves The*

Curlew by William Butler Yeats, is less trilling and sonorous than melancholic and moaning – hence the admonition by the poet that the bird's "crying brings to my mind / [the] passion-dimmed eyes and long heavy hair" of a lost love.

Many of the other sounds you experience in the bog are unfamiliar, even ominous-seeming, particularly when they ring out from within the marshland mists. They are the humming and buzzing of various bugs, such as crickets and dragonflies, and the malevolent drone of mosquitoes. Frogs and toads emit their belch-like repetitions, and there are frequent splashes and splooshes as creatures enter and exit the pools amidst the ponderous, heavy heads of rushes. Watery slaps, plops, and gurgles, without any perceivable cause – much of the activity within a wetland remains curtained by weeds, grasses, and trees – are regular, and disconcerting to new human visitors.

However, what these insects and fauna, as well as the myriad flora species that perpetuate and populate here, have in common, is what they grow from: *sludge. Muck. Mud.* The guttural 'u' consonants – considered a 'low' sound in English – intimate that this is a crude, crass thing. Yet what comes from it are marvels, proof positive that the most beautiful blooms grow from the filthiest sediment. And, whilst the sounds that emerge from its throats and thickets might seem strange, scary or sad, it is by stepping into this realm and allowing those emotions to arise within us from our projection – because, really, the wetlands are no more melancholic or miserable than anywhere else, it is only our perception that makes them so – that we can engage in our own healing. We know, now, that that desolate shriek is not Nellie Longarms but the whinnying of a furious little grebe; but the sound still produces in us a feeling of fear, and we can use this reaction to our advantage.

I have found that stepping into mudflats and mires has assisted in the processing of long-suppressed feelings and helped to root out negative emotional tendencies. The wetlands have acted as a mirror: to myself; to my body; to the emotional 'mud' within. Its cries and my own have mingled as I've trekked, fallen, entangled myself in bracken, stepped in pools that turned out to be rivers, been snagged, been bitten, almost tripped into an adder's nest, gotten lost. But still, here, I am definitely not a dog – I am a wolf. I let myself off the leash. I forget what I should be, and *be*. I grunt as I trudge through the mud, relishing the guttural 'u's of this action, and revelling in the strange, fantastical birdsong around me. I hum and sing, whistle and shout, emit the odd swear when I stumble. If, when I peer into the murky pools and puddles of the wetlands, I see myself, then it's in her strange and spooky sonics that I hear myself, too. Men, like mud, may belch and burp, and here those sounds are natural, not negative. The wind in these watery places accounts for much of the unusual soundscape, and often, it howls. It incites a howl in us – if not from us – too.

Like Dylan Thomas's description of nearby Swansea city, the terrain shifts from ugly-funny to 'ugly-lovely' when you walk through it. Furthermore, it reflects the ugly-loveliness of me; the ugly-loveliness of you; the ugly-loveliness of our voices, when they sing and cry and shriek, and of all our possible feelings, including those that we dismiss or designate 'negative', such as jealousy, loneliness, anger, and despair. A bog, fen, or marsh isn't a swamp of sadness, like in the film *Labyrinth*, but it allows us to feel sadness; and, by immersing into that feeling, we emerge from the swamp freed from it. The mud of our wetlands is emotionally cleansing, therefore, just as much as it is cleansing of rivers and catchments (an important ecological function of all such habitats). It is a kind of transmutation, and it is magic. The miracle of muck, mulch, and the mire, is that our bodies are, quite literally, swamped in it when we go wetland-walking; but our spirits, like wetland birds – or like their high and haunting cries – rise free.

Chapter 4

Blind-worm / adder's fork

Snakes are scary. In Wales and the UK, we're lucky not to have any animals or insects that are very poisonous. Still, the snake symbolises evil, an association embedded within our culture by the dualism of Christianity. A snake is a tempter, a servant of the Devil, if not the Devil himself. I remember reading, once, that God made some animals, and the Devil made others – all the more troublesome critters, like goats, which are far more boisterous, we feel, than sheep; and of course all the ugly, frightening, or potentially dangerous creatures, like spiders and serpents, beetles and bats. The creatures you find in many British wetlands, essentially. Put them all together, and you've got the *Llamhigyn Y Dwr*, or 'water leaper', a Welsh mythical creature which possesses the head of a toad, the body of a snake (including a sting in its tail), and the wings of a bat. Needless to say, it lives in swamps, and is considered evil in the extreme.

My partner wouldn't be scared of such a thing. They have always possessed an adventurous nature, having been introduced to hiking, hillwalking, and even mountain climbing by their father at a young age. They joke that I am like one of Doctor Who's Daleks, as I find it difficult to manage on uneven ground. And, it's true – I was raised a townie, and my feet aren't used to the slip and slide of loose soil or scree. It's been quite the journey, learning to trust my own legs. Sometimes, I've even slid back down very steep hills on my bottom, wishing I was a snake at those times and could do the job more quickly. If I were a mediaeval witch, maybe I could shape-shift in order to try and achieve that...! As it is, most of my spiritual adventures have been mystical or meditative rather than strictly occult in nature. I've never cast a spell (except, sometimes, by accident), preferring to attempt things 'directly', without word or action, item or assistance. Help in the form of spirits, angels, gods, and other entities *has* been involved, but I always spoke to these aides inwardly, in plain language, and never 'invoked' them, though they did turn up. I suppose I am very lucky for this, although I do have past lives as a witch (and in other spiritual roles – alongside other lives that were less spiritually focused, of course) to thank.

In this life, all that 'upwards stuff' has, for me, come pretty easily, as a result – it's the body, the emotions, grounding myself, being of the earth, that I've found most difficult. As a young person, I felt like a floating head, unattached to a large lump of meat; I cruelly ignored everything below the neck for many years. When I finally got around to the necessary self work, much of it was body-based, my physical form acting as a map for the other, less dense 'energy bodies'; and many of the blocks, knots, and issues I discovered took, in my mind's eye, the form of these 'evil creatures' – spiders, worms, and snakes.

The essence of everything in existence is, in my experience, a seed, which is also a flame, which is also an ocean, and it is conscious, and it is made up of 'light and love' – but, I don't live there, though I've been fortunate enough to find the way and sometimes make a visit. I live in this world, of blood, sweat and tears (and beauty, pleasure, and joy!), and I am a creature of it; hence, snakes are a cultural symbol that I've inherited, too, and generally for me they've been representative of blocks and similar in my energy system.

So, not 'evil' – useful, actually. These snakes have marked the way. They've assisted in my healing. And, generally, in my energetic practices and self-healing, they have transmuted, or been dissolved. The great Hindu god Shiva wears a snake wrapped at his neck, much like a familiar, and I see it as great and good. Vāsuki is this snake's name, and he is considered a god in Hindu culture. He sits about the human-esque god's beautiful blue body like a living amulet. In Wales, it's said that druids would wear an amulet which could only be found amongst a gathering of adders, usually in spring and most particularly on May Eve. This stone is glassy smooth, with a hole in it which some tales say is made by an adder's tongue, others by the sting in its tail. The *Glain Neidr* ('glain' = glass, 'neidr' = snake) was worn on a chain around the neck, and thought to provide powers of healing, protection, and prophecy. Wearers might also be blessed with the ability to become invisible, find hidden treasure, or else be victorious in battle. Another Welsh name for this prized charm was 'Maen Magl', or spotted stone ('magl' comes from the Latin meaning spot, speckle, or blemish), and it's also variously known as snake stone, adder's stone, adder's egg or, interestingly, hag stone, with which I'm sure most of us will be familiar.

If you are a magical or energetic practitioner, then I think you will agree that there is a particular energy to be found in these stones, and I believe, this stems not from snakes but more from the fact that the stone is 'true' if the hole is made without human direction or intent (Roud, 2006). I would encourage you to find such a stone and give it an energetic 'feel' to see what you can discern. In any case, it's unsurprising that the druids attributed this unusual stone to adders, as they were considered in a far more positive light than snakes are today. To them, the serpent symbolised the ability of humans to change, transform, and regenerate, due to the fact that the creatures shed their skins. My magickal experience of snakes (as visions in healing and meditation, rather than through physically foraging in bushes and thickets) has been the same – they represent our potential for transformation. Every snake I've encountered on the inner plane has been a pathway to some form of transmutation. They have been gatekeepers of change. In snakes and ladders we slide down the snakes, but in my experience serpents also possess the properties of ladders, leading us upwards on our path.

Wetlands are a wormy sort of place which may, again, come as no surprise. I would love to see a snake – my partner has heard one hissing and slithering "for a long time" (which means it was probably the UK's biggest serpent, a grass snake), and we are often on the lookout on our walks to try and spot them. However, we've yet to do so, but in their stead are plenty of other long-bodied friends: caterpillars, centipedes, earthworms, and slowworms. My first encounter with slowworms was as a child, when some bigger boys (I was perhaps 8 years old, they were maybe 12) threw one into our front garden to try and scare me. I responded, not by shrieking (although the size of the worm was quite frightening) but by putting on a nonchalant front as if I didn't care at all. The boys, disheartened by my lack of reaction, ambled away, disappointed, and I can't remember now how the worm ever left the garden. Certainly I didn't want to touch it…

Machismo and the male sex may be embodied by the snake. The bog, being full of concave pools, may be designated female. The French writer and theorist Hélène Cixous has written about this binary, male-female duality that's embedded within language and culture, and we project it onto nature, too. In wetlands, the phallic snake and the vulvic pond coexist side by side, and there are snakes in the ponds, too, in the form of eels. Wetlands, to me, are again an opportunity to transmute, this time in our view of the snake, not just from evil to good, but away from an evil phallus to an appendage that is helpful and useful. The snake is undeniably evil in Christianity partly because it resembles the male organ; but the penis is no more evil than its female counterpart. It's sex itself – conjugation; coupling – that Christianity has vilified; female bodies have been seen as sinful because sex has been projected onto them, causing them to become objectified as sexual items, and the penis has also been smothered in shame. There are repressive veins in other religions, but this is the one culturally embedded here, and it's still problematic. It is a further inheritance, of sorts, and one which, like other inherited issues – including that of the environmental crisis and climate change – we need to work now to solve. The earth's body, with its 'filthy' pools and 'dirty' snakes, its hags and devils – and us, viewing ourselves as filthy whores and dirty pervs if we just want to enjoy our own bodies and sharing them with others – demands this.

Let's remember, then, that in some other mythologies snakes are restorative. Shiva may seem culturally distant to those in some English-speaking countries (although there are Hindu communities and temples all around the UK, including in Wales), but we are familiar with the symbols composed of staff and snakes, and we know that these represent healing. The first staff is the *Rod of Asclepius*, belonging to the Greek god of healing and medicine. His staff is wrapped with a single serpent. We know, too, that snakes were used in rituals honouring Asclepius, as they were considered holy. The serpent of kundalini energy, snaking its way up the spine, is supposed to wind its way up the 'staff' of the spine in this same way. My own experience of kundalini has felt similar to a snake, making its way either languidly or in lightening-fashion when it isn't coiled in wait at the base of those bones.

The second staff is carried by the Greek god Hermes; it's called the caduceus, and consists of two snakes winding their way around the staff, which possesses, at its peak, wings. It is associated with the Greek god Mercury, and said to possess various powers. One of these stems from a myth involving Tiresias, who came across two copulating snakes. He killed the female with his staff, and for his crime was transformed into a woman. The staff, after this, retained transformative powers. The poet Penelope Shuttle beautifully encapsulates the magickal iconography inherent in the snake's stick-like form in her poem *Snake*: "Creature more magic than mouse or rat, / more thoughtful than donkey or cat, / ... You are only one skein, one thumb, / you are a long thin silver skin, / a rod that works for god" (Shuttle, 2012).

I find it interesting, too, that snakes, without very obvious male-female differences to the untrained eye, can seem quite asexual, fluid not just in motion but even in their sex. Earthworms, that we generally consider to be so lowly, looking down from our lofty human state, are of course hermaphrodite, possessing both male and female sex organs, and are, therefore, very magickal creatures indeed. They also 'eat dirt', quite literally, which is amazing to me – drawing nutrients from the earthy loam – and are regenerative to a degree, with the ability to grow a new tail if they are chopped in two. Another poet, Gail McConnell, writes in a poem entitled *Worm*: "Eyeless, your appetite aerates. / Eating the world, you open it" (McConnell, 2018). The worm, in her fine poem, elegantly creates even as it destroys, eating earth and enriching it with what it then passes out. To be called 'a worm' doesn't seem much of an insult in my eyes. In fact, it's quite the compliment! And I can think of very few more apt analogies for the essence of energetic healing, either – spinning shit into gold! – whatever name you happen to call it by.

Animals in the physical realm have acted as totems and omens, 'signs and wonders', consistently throughout my spiritual journey. They are one of the greatest marvels, appearing here and there to offer a message, a warning, an encouragement, or even a welcome (particularly where they have acted as a precursor to an encounter with an animal form deity on the inner plane). Worms and snakes are as much a part of this as any other creature. What can we learn from them? We know that the worm is a creature of transmutation; of regeneration; of beautifully amorphous sexuality. Snakes shed their old skins, moving deftly from one outmoded form to another, growing beyond their old form. Worms, in the form of caterpillars, also transmute, changing form entirely, and these abound in the rich, life-giving wetlands. There is potentiality and there is learning in all these things.

Cinnabar moths make
caterpillars that strike
like matches: stripes
of orange and black on
poison ragwort. Poison

themselves, the plump,
sweetie-fat things wriggle
like babies, safe in the
fact of their own toxicity.
They are lit so bright:

brazen chubbsters
munching on horse-killer
green; tiny tumtums
tramuting death into
their own second life.

Then, there are those snakes with wings – dragons. I don't think, in myth, the wetlands are naturally a home to these creatures, but there are dragonflies, which in Welsh are *gwas y neidir* – the adder's serpent. Wetlands are home to grass snakes rather than adders, but there are plentiful numbers of dragonflies, which in summer rule over ponds like soldiers, skimming the air on their circuits, dazzling in their colours and buzzing in snakish imitation. Dragonflies possess many other folk names, including *flying dragon*. They're as close as we'll get to such beings in the swamp, but their brightness and their brilliance marks them out against this glib, glum backdrop. Dragonfly and damselfly larvae take years to gestate, living then as glittering airborne beings for a few weeks or months, and they are truly one of the greatest sources of wonder on a summer visit to the bog. No wonder that these insects possess many names, and are so rich in association. They inspire the soul, when you see them. Some of these names and tales tell us that *spinning Jenny* – one of dragonfly's English aliases – is also a servant of not just the adder but the Devil himself (who of course takes snake's form), and has the power to see through to our soul, and to judge it.

Spinning Jenny sits in air, a sky-sire, a fire-gem;
a little arrow, weigher of souls, the devil's darting needle.

Speak wrong and her stitching tail will come to tie your tongue.
Speak right and she'll pass you by, glittering like a sword.

Instrument of devil or lord, we agree that she is ether.
Gwas y neidir, adder's serpent, the tempter's busy minion,

snake doctor, *ether mon*, flying dragon, silverpin.
Her names are as myriad as any immortal being.

But her buzz comes as a warning, a hum of impending end.
Her traffic light colours of amber and red signal that we should stop.

For we are entering an extinction event, the ending of the Earth.
And spinning jenny – the balance fly, the kiteflee, the spindle,

iridescent as an Egyptian locust, a scarab of the air –
will one day point her tail our way. Will one day weigh our souls.

Back down in the mire, one the most numerous worm-like creatures in local wetlands has always been the eel. Eels were, at one point in our history, actually considered a currency in their own right, being so very plentiful in wetland provinces.

Where there have been wetlands, there have, historically, been people – it's only in recent times that we've come up out of the swamp, as it were. In the past, our ancestors naturally chose to locate themselves in mudflats and peatlands, since "the twin ecosystems of coastal estuary and freshwater swamp provided a continual bounty of edible plants, fish, birds, shellfish and mammals...[and] marsh-dwellers had access to sediment-rich grazing and cropping grounds during the drier months to complement the wild food supply" (Boyce, 2021). Eels were a natural food source and when, later, it came time to pay tithes to local church and state, in some areas of Britain eels were accepted in lieu of coin. Many other wormy creatures were consumed, too. Far away, on the Nile, the cobra-headed Renenutet was considered the goddess of nourishment and fertility, with a responsibility for overseeing the raising and rearing of children, as well as the harvest, and although there's no equivalent deity here the water-land was often revered for its life-giving qualities.

Yet, as I say, we've left behind all that nasty mud, and can now simply gather up our supplies from the sterile shelves of the supermarket, or even have them delivered. We don't need to forage in the fens any longer. There's no impetus to go catching any mucky, slimy eels; and, in fact, due to our changes in farming methods and the outpouring of pollution we've engendered, eels are no longer in such plentiful supply. In a sense, we've elevated ourselves, from worms to dragons – grown wings, and are able to fly (which we can also now do literally, of course). We're not blind-worms, down in the dirt, any more. But we've lost so much learning, so much connection, in that process, and have even endangered the Earth itself. I would argue that we've *become* blind worms, blinkered to not just the real value of wetlands but everything in nature. All ground has been rendered 'dirt' in this un-seeing; all life-giving, fruit-bearing ground is 'filth'. We forget that, like the earthworm, we need that dark, dirty stuff for our food, just the same. We forget that, like the snake, we are creatures of change, transformation, and renewal, and that the 'things' we class as resources are also alive, of the Earth, with a similar need to renew. It's time, now, to refresh our vision of the world, and our own place in it; to take off our blinkers, and stop being worms – or less than worms – before it's too late.

Chapter 5

In the cauldron

The wetlands are still terrains that are rich in plentiful food sources; not that we readily know that, these days. We tend to view nature as retaining a 'use', either ornamental or practical, a thing for our eyes or our mouths; although at various times there's incredible beauty to be found in the bog, we have become disconnected from it as a feeding ground and provider of fish and fowl. At one historical site – a settlement near Cat's Water wetlands – over twenty types of bird bone were found, including "mallard, pelican, cormorant, heron, stork, mute swan, barnacle goose, teal, table duck, merganser, sea eagle, goshawk, buzzard, crane, coot and crow" (Boyce, 2021), in a manner that made plain that these were a vital source of vittles, and fish, eels, and other of the gelatinous creatures of the swamp were also regularly consumed. The friend who introduced me to the wetlands I now live next to took me, later, for an hour's forage across the small, grassy strip that lies next to the more watery area, and in that time – and in an area that might, usually, take under five minutes to traverse – we found myriad sorts of flower and leaf, herb and seed: enough for a gorgeous and colourful wild salad.

There's something fulfilling about finding your own food and picking it yourself; the ritual, then, of washing, slicing, arranging in a dish. It tastes better; more nourishing, somehow. I've made jam from berries gathered at the edge of the marsh, too, and pies from the blackberries on that strip opposite my house. A spurt of wild mint poking from the wall like a green tongue provides cups of pale, refreshing tea. There are fine purple borage flowers and yellow dandelion suns, all edible, along with our common, much overlooked daisy. Its white wheel makes for a fine addition to any salad, and is a lovely little reminder of how even the everyday, very common sorts of plant and flower around us, stepped on or over numerous times, in fact possess numerous properties. Not that we need to eat the world, but the simple fact of a daisy's culinary ability seems to transmute the ordinary into the marvellous. What else abounds in the nearby wetlands – or anywhere else in nature for that matter – which we've lost all knowledge of? What are the nearby alternatives to fruits and vegetables shipped from other continents, or herbs processed and packed in the far east or distant south, which we can gather ourselves? Not only does this reduce our carbon footprint and fuel emissions, not only is this practice mindful as well as meditative, but it just feels *really good*.

Ceridwen, in Welsh mythology, is an enchantress, sometimes a goddess, who possesses a magical cauldron. In this, there might exist a brew of transformation or inspiration. The legendary bard, Taliesin, is said to have (eventually! It's a long story) emerged into the world thanks to its powers. In some ways, I see the wetlands here as a cauldron, with gifts of inspiration and transformation to show, teach, offer up. A cauldron is an implement in which many ingredients are gathered, as they are here, where a richesse of plant and animal life abounds. The mouth of the cauldron is one which, in the wetlands, replaces that of the hungry, human-eating Nelly Longarms and Peg Grindylow; it gives life instead of stealing it away.

The inspiration that Ceridwen's cauldron gives includes *awen*, poetic inspiration, which is also in abundance in the fen. Perhaps there are very few marsh or bog poems, but there are plenty of poems that look to the estuary, which is where rivers meet the sea and mud and marshland are never too far away. If you've ever paid a visit to Laugharne, the famous estuary home of the Welsh poet Dylan Thomas, you'll see clearly the inspiration of estuary shining through in his verse. Those poems take herons and moonlight as their images, rather than slowworms and silt – how much more poetic those silvery emblems are than anything mud-bound! – but it's estuary none the less, with great, ever-present mud banks that gleam wetly beneath the low sun. Since the Severn's tidal range is one of the greatest in the world (and this is the same river which runs past my own house, too), it's an epic expanse, impressive to behold. I envy Dylan his boathouse home overlooking the mud, marsh, and water. A poet can only aspire to such things!

I've been to Laugharne many times, more times than I can count, and the view out over the water never fails to inspire. There are boatfuls of *awen* here. The wetland feeds our soul, even as it feeds our mouths. Both pens and bellies may be filled with it. I'm sure the more witchy amongst you will be interested in the herbs and flowers of wetlands, and their various magical properties, but since wetlands are so diverse and situated in so many countries around the world, it would require much more space than I have been allowed here to discuss this. If you'd like to know more, then I'd suggest a little research and of course a field trip to your own local swamp to learn and make your own discoveries (bearing in mind that the mud realms near you might be home to creatures that are more dangerous than the ones we have here in Wales – along the Nile, the crocodile headed deities Sobek and Ammit rule as king and queen, with good reason, as these creatures swim there, and they may do near you, too).

My best advice, on any field trip, would be to observe the plants and flowers and make a preliminary enquiry into their nature later at home if they are unfamiliar to you. Some plants in wetlands are rare and must not be picked. Generally, I feel that we should not do so anyway – wildflowers and plants need all the space they can get. Additionally, under the UK's *Wildlife and Countryside Act* (1981), it's illegal to uproot wild plants without the permission of the landowner or occupier – although gathering leaves, fruit, seeds and stems is fine. Other plants are deadly poisonous, and easily mistaken for lookalikes which are edible. So, when you enter this fertile cauldron, take care to remember that not everything here is a potential 'ingredient' and, indeed, it would be wrong to bring that 'consumer eye' into the wetlands (as much as I love foraging myself) and to have it as your primary reason for being here, particularly when we've depleted wetlands so much and disregarded their green bounty in favour of the sheen of bank notes.

Still, if you love to forage, and are mindful of the fact that wetlands have been reduced in size and are a little more fragile than they once were, then finding food is possible and is a wonderful way of connecting to the earth and water here. I never was very interested in the 'feminine art' of cooking, because to me it never seemed an art but more of a chore tied to the chains of enforced domesticity. That doglike sense that I've written about in part came from this, no doubt, too. Women have long been kept – kennelled – at home. Every adventure book I read as a child featured a male in the lead, whilst a woman sat at home keeping things neat for his eventual return. I always identified with the lead, and only at puberty sadly realised that I was born the wrong sex for adventure, historically at least. Things have – and continue to keep – changing, but old ideas of women and women's place (and men and men's place!) are still sadly ingrained in our culture.

For this reason, I consciously rejected cooking and all other 'womanly' practices and interests from a young age. I never had any baby dolls or dressing up dolls, apart from a couple of Cabbage Patches (because they were ugly!) and a Jem doll, who was a cool, 1980s version of Sindy and Barbie, but with her own business and no need for a Ken. I certainly never had any kitchen or food preparation toys, although I liked drinking pretend tea with my sister and having make believe parties. I didn't identify as 'female' with regards to particular interests. I believe these to be mostly assigned to us rather than innate in any case: men can be motherly and women can be adventurous; men can be soft, sensitive and gentle, and women can be commanding and authoritative, in my experience. In the past lives I remember, I have been a mix of both male and female, and in one lifetime, as a kind of temple dancer, I feel myself then and there as neither – a girlish boy or a boyish girl, somehow. Although my energy and interests in this life are very typically female in some ways – I love dresses, jewellery, and perfume, for example! – I've always felt my inner self to be without sex. My 'thoughts' are not female. My heart and my soul are not. When I think 'I' there isn't a body there, and no physical, sex-specific attributes to assign. I'm not even an earthworm, with both characteristics – somehow, I am neither. When you think 'I', in the deepest sense possible, don't you feel yourself the same way, too...?

In any case, it's been a joy to come to the wetlands and feed from this cauldron from time to time; as anyone of any sex or gender, age or background, can. I've felt a kind of cauldron, too, in the kundalini energy which bubbles now and then at the base of my spine. With that cauldron brewing, and the cauldron of the wetlands brewing its inspiration as well, the wetlands have provided many lovely and memorable times, not just in their beauty and bounty but in energy and creative impetus. Earth-based energy work is of course something you might naturally wish to engage with, in this natural terrain, and connecting to earth is something I would encourage you to practice daily, wherever you are, but it's an urge that's particularly inspired by wild surroundings I feel. There's also the potential, here, for animal signs and symbols and for those who read / see / are offered patterns and images in things (I never know which one it is – whether I am actively 'seeing', or passively being 'shown' – it always feels like a magical gift when these things appear to me!) I find that the repeating grasses, hedges, leaves, and sunlight speckles on water, are particularly good for this and for gaining psychic visions / glimpses / symbols and related spiritual insights.

Additionally, some of you might wish to explore the 'in-between' nature of wetlands in a deeper way. Their rich mythology includes will-o'-the-wisps, a ghostly ball of light seen in swamps, bogs and marshes all around the world, including the UK, USA, and Europe. Whether these are myth, or whether they are something else – nature spirits, fae or, as some legends posit, the souls of the dead – is up to you to discover. I've not personally encountered a will-o'-the-wisp, but the fact that they cross many cultures makes them highly interesting. Where there are bogs, there are these ethereal bog entities, whatever they might be. My own encounters with human spirits have tended to be in the built-up places they once, when they were embodied, inhabited, particularly their homes, as you'd expect of any human being; in terms of other entities, nature spirits are a distinct possibility, although I'm not a particular favourite of the fae, so to speak! Another explanation is that they are, perhaps, some sort of bioluminescence, and since wetlands are very damp places that, too, is possible. Bioluminescence and nature spirits are not mutually exclusive, of course, but whether you 'see' with your eyes or your 'eye' is of course personal and particular to you.

Some writers suggest that, due to their 'in-between' nature, wetlands may act as portals or gateways to other worlds. Whether this is so is, again, up to the more magically inclined amongst you to determine. What's for certain is that bogs are rich in so many elements, from physical foods and herbs to a multitude of myths and stories; incredible beauty and poetic inspiration to plenty of magical possibilities. They are brilliantly biodiverse locales, too, many of them existing at the edge of cities in Wales and the UK simply because our ancestors were able to feed themselves so readily from them. As such, they tended to settle here. And so, some of the wetlands near to me are easily accessible; only a short walk away; only just around the bend. In the wetlands opposite my house, the sound of the nearby link road adds an ever present, white noise hum; the creatures and features there thrive in spite of it; and it's another aspect to the many other aspects that exist, intertwined, here. Whether you are irritated by the sound or use it as a means of merging ever more mindfully into your immediate environment is up to you. Mysticism, in my experience, must happen in the everyday, amidst the mundane and life's many small distractions and annoyances, or not at all. Here's another opportunity, in my view, to practice, and to sharpen our intent.

This is a cauldron plushly full with plentiful ingredients – harbouring a "rich soup of life", as a recent news article about the Gwent Levels in Wales proclaimed (Morris, 2022) – and whether your aim is sustenance or spirituality, inspiration or relaxation, there is enough stuff here to feed you. I urge you to step into these fertile habitats and discover this for yourself.

Chapter 6

Toe of Frog

A cauldron is a perfect receptacle for transformation; it is both a vessel and a vehicle of change – in it, ingredients transmogrify from plain and practical, unprocessed and prosaic (leaf, stem, seed) to creations with properties beyond those held by any one constituent part alone. Whether you bake a cake or blend a potion, this physical process is the same, and the cauldron – the cooking pot – remains a magical implement in any kitchen. Turning a bag of old carrots, some limp celery from the bottom of the fridge, and a misshapen onion into a delicious soup (as I did last night) is one kind of alchemy. Creating an enchanted potion is another. And immersing yourself in nature's cauldron, and letting it work its magic on you, is yet another again.

In fairytales, characters nearly always transform. The poor girl who is treated as a dog ends the story by becoming a princess; the frog who belches up from the bottom of a well is later revealed as a prince. In our own lives, we are worked upon by processes myriad and multiple, whether we are conscious of them or not, and are, as a result, in a constant flux of change. In my own life, I felt 'stuck' for a very long time as a young person, and then the magic of energy work, self healing, and poetry came, like a fairy godmother, to set me 'free'. That admixture acted as a kind of medicine, really. However, that stuck sense was an inner feeling; in reality, I was changing continuously, from child to teen, teen to adult, and as a result of untold interactions, instances, and imprints. My mind changed; my manners changed; my opinions and ambitions changed. Life is far more fluid than the narratives we tell ourselves and the templates we hold in our minds. The subconscious and the superconscious also have their parts to play, and are affected by energies and understandings which our conscious mind often fails to articulate or even comprehend.

We change, just as all other animals change. A tadpole turns into a frog. Is it the same creature? Its heart remains essentially the same, but its outward form is entirely different. It leaps from element to element, morphing from water-bound to air-breathing, a creature of earth, eventually, as well as water. Amphibians are perhaps the most appropriate symbol of swamp, combining those same two elements of earth and air as they do, intermingling them and managing to embody both. There are various types of frog and toad to be found in wetlands places, from native species such as common frog, common toad, and pool frog, to marsh frogs and other non-native breeds. Toads in particular are a wonder to behold. These great, granular-skinned kings wear their warts grandly, and do not ask to be transformed into a smooth-skinned prince. They sit, unblinking, amidst the mud and grass, and when they move around they walk, strolling as if they own the place (which they do), unlike their frog counterparts, who jump. They are flatter than frogs, and darker, so that they blend in more readily with soil and sediment than grass, and are more easily camouflaged. They are lumps of muck with eyes, mounds of mud come to life – if ever any creature was a real life *Boglin*, then old toady is most certainly it.

As is the way with so many marshland creatures, these veer from silly to sinister. Frogs are funny. If you call someone a frog, the meaning might be that they are awkward, clumsy, or something similar, with 'frog legs' and an ungainly gait, but certainly they are non-threatening. Think of all the frogs in our culture, from to Harry Potter chocolates to *The Muppet Show*'s Kermit – they're cute, foolish, sweet. On one of the shelves at home growing up, my mother had a series of ornamental brass frogs, sitting, singing, acting the clown. Frog is a gangly green fool. Toads are more malevolent. If you call someone a toad, you're inferring that they're ugly, and more besides – that they are repellant, either physically, morally, in their manners, or in some other sense; perhaps, even, in all of them. A witch's familiar might be a toad, although in the Christian Bible frogs are also an evil magick, appearing en masse as one of the ten plagues of Egypt.

Both are redolent with negative connotations, therefore, whilst, as with the snake, in other places and at other times frogs and toads were venerated. Alongside the snake god and goddess of ancient Egypt sat Heqet, a toad-headed deity who was the embodiment of fertility. No wonder, when you think of the massy glob of eggs that a single frog or toad can lay – up to around 4,000 in one go. Each year, when the Nile flooded – a regular occurrence in estuary wetlands – it provided water for distant fields, and was, therefore, of huge benefit to agriculture. Since frogs at this time also appeared in great numbers, being deposited on the river's muddy banks and further afield in bogs, they became linked to this essential surge, and so were seen as a symbol of abundance. The Aztecs also venerated the frog, in the form of "a goddess known as Ceneotl, the patron of childbirth and fertility, who took the form of a frog or a toad with many udders" (Lee, 2019), as well as the toad, Tlaltecuhti, "the earth mother goddess, who embodied the endless cycle of death and rebirth" (Lee, 2019).

The 'double life' of these amphibians naturally makes them redolent with relative symbolism. Like snakes, they signify transformation, regeneration, and renewal. Further than this, the two lives of frogs and toads have been seen as symbolic of our own incarnated, physical life, and discarnate, spiritual life that some of us understand as preceding it, existing within the physical, and then coming as its inevitable prologue. For those with no conscious or remembered experience of the spiritual realm, or who choose to hold the belief of non-belief regarding these, then frogs and toads may still symbolise our twin lives, but in other senses: as physical creatures / conscious creatures; as living creatures who come from nothing, and who later return to nothing as dead or inanimate matter.

Last spring, I was able to witness the early stages of the frog life cycle, both as spawn and, on a sunny afternoon later in the year, as hundreds if not thousands of tadpoles swimming for their lives. Only a small number of these would have made it to froglet, and then to their subsequent frog form. Therefore, tadpoles represent potentiality – the struggle to be, to grow, to fully evolve and become all that we can become. In meditation, especially in my more puritanical and morally rigid younger years, this would always be the dedication / request I would make before beginning – 'help me become all I can become, in the highest sense, so that I may be of assistance to all other creatures...'. It isn't a bad thing, but in middle age I am less inclined to 'ask' for things – even very lofty things like becoming a Boddhisatva! – than to just sit, accept, and 'be'. I've made it beyond my desperate, wriggling tadpole form, and am now a happy, contented froglet. I don't need to swim for survival any more, although I do yearn to find a nice (lily) pad on which to make myself a home. I think if frog has anything to teach me now, at this age, then it's that, even if I do make myself a home (being settled in a property I own seems most important to me at the current time), life's inherent brevity, and subsequent uncertainty, means that we are always, in some sense, 'on the hop'. We dream of our own place or space, and build ourselves nests as best we can; but always, beneath them, waters shift, never settled, despite the pool's appearance of stillness... For the nature of water is movement; and the nature of life is the same.

I have found the qualities and concepts that frog represents to be the most difficult for me. Transformation has not come naturally, and I find change generally quite difficult. Perhaps because of my childhood, I seem to lack a certain inner resilience. I am unsettled by small things – any tiny disruption to my personal pond – and shy away from others as a result. I can be awkward and ungainly – two of the negative aspects of frog – even appearing rude when, like an amphibian, I am startled and make an unexpected conversational 'hop'. I am too direct at these times, throwing myself at the person I am talking to; leaping violently in a kind of defensiveness. I often have a metaphorical frog in my throat at those moments – speech generally was a real issue for me when I was younger, as I've said – and so I spit it up. The words emerging from my mouth become a sort of plague, raining down upon whoever I am speaking with. Shyness might be a good word for it, except in some situations – situations where I am in charge, and where my role is clearly defined e.g. as teacher – I'm not shy at all. I become an all-singing, all-dancing, entertaining frog. Kermit would definitely be proud!

The frog is also a symbol of fertility. My issues with my body have been around this, centred in the sexuality and femininity of my form. Frogs copulate in a position known as *amplexus*, in which the male positions himself on the back of the female and grasps her. I remember seeing this image, perhaps on television, as a child, and being appalled. It was the grasping, grabbing nature of it that seemed so awful to me – the capturing by the male, and the being squatted upon. I never, ever wanted to be grabbed, gained, or even 'won', as a fairy tale princess might be. I never wanted to be treated as an object, whether that was a trifle or a trophy. Abuse meant that I held complex thoughts around sex and submission for a very long time, and as a younger person avoided all real-life romantic attachments.

Strangely, I was, from a very young age, extremely romantic in my imagination, and one of the first songs I ever owned was *The Frog Song* by Paul McCartney. Its cartoon pop video, with imagery of gentlemen frogs and lady frogs, king frog and queen, really appealed to me. But this genteel, ordered hierarchy isn't the reality – a few years later, frogs were on our workbenches in school, murdered and splayed, pinned to a board and ready for us to dissect in biology class. That cosy, soft focus video, and the brutal reality of an IRL frog, killed and sliced, its legs wide whilst its belly was scissored, its innards shining and spilling out, spoke volumes to me. Myth and reality, idea and fact, the smoke of our mental imaginings and the reality of our brutal physical realm, were made terribly clear, and my mind sharpened like a scalpel to embrace these dichotomies, dismissing romance as rubbish even as, frog-like, some very sentimental and immature part of me clung to that concept.

This romantic notion was some bad sustenance I could never truly let go of. I always was an idealist, and this idea of boy-girl coupling was very deeply embedded. Although I rejected motherhood – including 'motherhood as play' – from a young age, and proclaimed to hate romcoms and typically romantic things when a little older, I didn't really. At school, I was always best at 'pair work', and have long felt that being part of a couple would really suit me, offering me the right balance of support, intimacy, and affection that I need. I think that letting go of romantic fantasies and expectations in favour of a more pragmatic and realistic approach to relationship has been a major learning point in my life (after I was able to even engage with others romantically, of course). The first film I ever saw in the cinema was *ET*, and the scene in which main character Eliot replays a scene from *Gone With The Wind* with a female classmate, as frogs escape from near dissection and hopped all around them, has stayed in my mind. It was romantic, and in that set piece it was linked to the idea that we humans have the power to free our trapped or enslaved fellow creatures. Our free hearts – full of love – want kisses, connection, and freedom; they want freedom and happiness for all other beings, too. How wonderful!

In reality, we can't always help others as we would like. Neither can we simply reenact archetypal roles without, very often, denying our own complexity. Frogs don't always turn out to be princes, either; toads might, despite your best efforts, remain exactly that. But who needs a prince in any case…? Fairytales are full of simple ideals, and I eventually realised that I needed to reject the 'male-female' duality of them if I wanted to escape their archetypes, which determine, too, that boys inherit kingdoms whilst girls wait to be won. The roles of boys are also limited, with sexism and sex-based stereotyping affecting, and limiting, all of us – can't boys be wooed and won, too…? All humans possess the potential to inhabit all roles, I feel, and no aspect of this social and cultural role-play should be denied to any of us.

In stories, a witch might turn someone into a frog as a punishment, too, but the ability to shape shift and live 'two lives' – as a human, then as an animal – would bring so much learning, I feel. It's only as frogs that characters in fairytales 'learn their lesson' and undergo personal transformation and change. So, it isn't a bad thing, perhaps, to be a frog; inside, you are still developing and growing – change remains continuous, even despite your fixed outward form. As well as potentially hiding the spirit of an enchanted human man or woman, it was once thought that toads, like snakes, also held a stone within them: "the toad, ugly and venomous, / Wears yet a precious jewel in his head" (Shakespeare). This 'toadstone', like the snake equivalent, was considered to possess powers such as the healing of tumours, cure of poisoning, and protection for newborn children (Duffin, 2010). Later, it was found that the stone we had come across in mud, and thought originated within the toad – to be coaxed from it by enticing it to cough up – was in fact a fossilised tooth belonging to a type of fish that was common hundreds of millions of years ago in the Jurassic and Cretaceous Periods.

In any case, for a time, we in Britain and Ireland believed the toadstone to be a magical instrument which came from the brain or belly of this wetland creature. I personally believe that it's the frog itself which is magical and, like all creatures, and all bodies (including our own) is to be revered. I wrote this short poem long before I'd ever read about toadstones or the gruesome methods used to extract the stone from its amphibian host. The ultimate magick, I feel, is not in the occult association of toads and frogs, but in the 'isness' of a breathing, living being which, like us, holds the seed-fire of life at its core. Here's the poem, in any case; short, maybe strange; but I felt this one emerged fully formed from me, and I cough it up here for your interest, amusement, or otherwise.

The green skin of the frog,
thin as thumbnail, holds inside
a heart as red as a volcano.

A tiny ruby, wrought within
an emerald, sitting, just there
upon the crystal of the world.

Chapter 7

Eye of Newt

Our human worldview holds humans at the centre of it. We are the toadstone in this particular green frog. Imagine a map – in the middle, we place ourselves. But that ant or bird or blade of grass or water droplet or even globule of mud has just as much right to exist as any of us. Nature is in no way dependant upon human beings for its survival. Nature encompasses us, and we are intertwined with her, but she is bigger than us; she existed before and, if we intend on destroying ourselves by making our habitat unfit for human life, then she will continue after we are gone. Some management may now be needed to help retain or maintain what we've impacted upon, it's true, and this is the case in wetland areas, but it's also true that our presence has proven detrimental to wildlife and plants in so many ways, across every acre of Earth, so much so that *not* being in a place is, in part, the remedy we need to internalise and utilise at this present moment.

So – *don't* take a walk to your local wetland, necessarily. Go there to learn, to immerse, to reconnect with the wild, but only when you feel a strong, soul-felt, utterly compelling need. I find it interesting that we often bemoan the presence of other humans when they crowd together in our wild places – yes, too many people trudging through a green area will trample and spoil it. However, we can't remove the other humans – the obvious solution is to remove ourselves. If you do visit a wetland habitat, then always, always make sure to stick to the prescribed paths, where they exist, as some of our local marshes do exist primarily as sanctuaries for birds, fish and wildflowers, and it can upset creatures or cause damage if we stray into their nesting, feeding, or mating zones. It's their home over and above our own, I feel, especially since we've hunted and harmed so many species beyond submission, into endangerment or even extinction. Many common birds are now, in the UK, on the 'red list' – also known as the *Birds of Concern* report – meaning that they are under threat, and this includes various wetland species such as the curlew, marsh tit, and marsh warbler. (The *IUCN Red List of Threatened Species* is its international equivalent, should you live outside of the UK.)

Let's *not* take our dog for a walk to these places, ideally, because they will unwittingly disrupt birds as they walk. It's the nature of a dog to hunt and chase smaller creatures, but we hold responsibility for this, as we hold the physical reins of the dog itself. As much of a dog lover as we might be, by allowing our pet free rein and letting it scare and disturb other animals in their homes, *we* are causing damage and continuing to disrupt wetlands and plunge them into danger and disarray. Our actions, on this micro level, mirror the greater disturbances that occur on the macro scale when developers hack into wetlands to create motorways and supermarkets. Whether it's a dog or a bulldozer, either way, we frighten birds and endanger their nesting, and some may be scared away permanently from an already fragile sanctuary space by such aggressive actions.

On a related side note: when a dog terrorises smaller animals, and the humans who own it let it, this isn't, to me, an act of 'affection' for nature. The human is letting a part of themselves attack smaller, defenceless, perhaps even endangered creatures. We need to take responsibility for what we do in and to nature, and this includes the nature of those creatures who we have brought more closely into our lives and society in the form of pets. If we have made wolves less wild and tamed them into dogs, then we can – and should – address their 'natural' behaviour when it comes to terrorising creatures we as a human species have forced into smaller numbers. We owe it to the Earth to retain her species, not to render them extinct, and this extends, now, to the part we allow our four legged friends to play in the narrative of nearly lost species. Let's not make these innocent pups our accomplices. The blood might be on their paws, literally, but in the greater sense it will actually be on our own.

If we are to create a 'Wetlands code of conduct', then I think it would be to

- STAY on paths where they exist and do not veer into any areas that are marked off.
- STEER away from breeding grounds, nests, and feeding areas for birds and other animals.
- STOP and think – do you really need to visit the wetlands, anyway?

Of course, I love wetlands and really enjoy visiting them; and I think it probable that the grey-brown muck-ness of such places means that they will never be as popular to visitors as our woods and beaches, especially in winter. However, I do always follow the code above, and as well as this I'm mindful of other codes, for example, *The Countryside Code* in Wales and the rest of the UK, which echoes my thoughts above: namely, that dogs should be kept "under control and in sight", and that we should "care for nature" and "not cause any damage or disturbance". I enjoy foraging, too, but in her book *The Hedgerow Handbook: Recipes, Remedies and Rituals*, Wales-based author and 'foraging guru' Adele Nozedar minds us not to over-do it, and my feeling after reading her wonderful book is that we should treat the wild world not as we do a supermarket but more as a nurturing body: bodies feel pain; bodies may be fat or thin, plentiful in their abundance, or hard, dry, bony, not able to give nourishment; bodies may have parts that are freely given, such as a hand, and others that are private and not ours to know: and I feel that this is a way of thinking that can translate into important guidelines for us to follow.

Being 'wild' isn't the same as being senseless, anarchic, or destructive, either; it's about existing and acting in a way that's in tune with nature and not overstepping bounds. There is a harmony that exists in the wild world; in the ebb and flow of its seasons, the mating and migration of its animals; in the gestation and germination of insects and flowers, that then, at the right time, unfurl from their encasements to buzz and bloom. Human creatures are now so out of touch with nature that we've lost this sense of seasonality; our basic needs – for food and water, warmth and shelter – and our success in creating machines and methods for maximising these, and making sure we have them consistently, has wildly unhinged us.

Eventually, these modes have in fact led to pollution of our water and food, through chemicals, pollutants, and waste. The deforestation that has occurred so that we can grab more land for farming and cattle is now endangering the very air we breathe, as the rainforests – 'the lungs of the earth' – create less and less oxygen each year, and people grow ill or even die from toxic air fumes in our most urbanised areas. Warmth and shelter, too, have led to further pollution, of deadly air borne gases that come from the burning of fossil fuels so we can live in comfort indoors. The land has been stripped of trees, metals, stone, and other elements, and natural places damaged or destroyed, so we can build more homes, more offices, more shops, more roads. The key word here is 'more', for there never seems to be an end to this building and blocking off of nature, with acres eaten every day, and concrete – the "most destructive material on Earth after water" (Watts, 2019) – replacing the nasty, oozy mud of earth in favour of this grey muck which we can, we believe, better control and confine. It rises daily, and it continues to rise.

As a result, wetlands have been harmed many times over. Seeming less 'enchanted' than a forest, and less 'mystical' than a mountain, they've been filched from and filled in, their bounty and biodiversity thoughtlessly forgotten. And so, their richness has been squandered, and in a short time slimmed down to a fraction of what it once was, to the point that we are losing – have lost – these precious habitats at an alarming rate. They might not be as magnificent as a rainforest, but wetlands have their own purpose – they are the 'kidneys of the earth', and serve a vitally important purpose in terms of filtration. They also hold carbon, provide flood control, and provide biodiversity in their myriad flora and fauna species (please see Chapter 10 for more on these).

The issue here, I feel, is that we value our ourselves too highly and all around us too little. We mistake wants for needs, and don't see any reason why we shouldn't have what we desire. Following lockdown, there were lots of news articles and posts on social media about people visiting beautiful wild places and leaving piles of rubbish there. Why? Because we literally don't see the value of nature; because our own small enjoyments are considered to be more important than the well-being of plants and animals. We have objectified nature so that we can only see it as food, water, shelter or warmth; but, now, necessity has expanded into greed, and has not been tempered by empathy – empathy for other creatures and for the natural world. We badly need to regain that connected sense, so that we know that when we harm nature, we harm ourselves. But how do we do this…?

I'm not sure that projecting ourselves onto the natural world is the final answer. We hold complex relationships with ourselves, for a start. And nature isn't our 'mirror' – it is Life, Life itself, in vital, vivid, vivacious and very varied form, and we are a part of it, not outside of it looking in. The language of poetry is very interesting in this respect. Recently, I made a radio programme about clouds. Very often, clouds in poetry are described in terms of simile, and nearly all of these similes put the clouds in human terms: clouds like pillows; clouds like baby's curls; clouds like mounds of mashed potato. We filter through a self-referencing lens, just as our ancestors saw gods and goddesses in the sun and moon. Not much has changed in this respect. Perhaps this process of projection comes naturally to us, and is a means of understanding the wild world, but we must move beyond this propensity, now we are aware of it, into a more mature and respectful way of seeing, I believe – a way of seeing that doesn't put us 'in' and at the centre of everything.

Indeed, psychologist Patricia Ganea asserts that "Anthropomorphism can lead to an inaccurate understanding of biological processes in the natural world" (Millman, 2022). It can lead children to retain less factual understanding about animals, instead encouraging them to retain fuzzy, fantastical 'facts' based upon cartoons and other entertainment. Nature itself becomes a kind of cartoon, filled with Jiminy Crickets, Winne-the-Poohs, and Simbas. Cultural / pop-culture representations of nature therefore become a barrier to natural connection; and then there's the added effect of 'connecting' via a screen, which is distant as well as distorted, as if animals, even in documentaries, are far, far away and not quite real, somehow. How can a child retain an empathy for nature if nature doesn't seem real to them...?

In a way, there will always exist a gulf between humankind and nature – put simply, nature doesn't need us. Nature would in fact be better off without us! But conversely, connecting with nature requires, I think, our immersion into it. We must, however, do this whilst bearing the recent wrongs of our near ancestors in mind. Over the past 200 years, particularly over the last 50, we've depleted the kingdom of flora and fauna, killing many species into extinction, never to be seen on Earth again, from the dodo to the ivory-billed woodpecker, declared extinct in 2021. The international day for lost species on November 30 each year is a recent addition to the calendar, but rather than a celebration it's a day of activism, reflection, and mourning. So, I think that yes, going into nature is still the answer, but we have to keep our huge population, our consumerist tendencies, and the wreckage we have already wrought, in mind, making sure our walks into the wild are light of foot, taking little or nothing, and even giving back where we can.

We must learn to see with the eye of nature – eye of newt, even. This greening eye is one that is entirely other to our own. It doesn't project itself onto nature; indeed, as a creature of camouflage, and a creature of both water and earth, it is an animal that invites us to do the same – to blend in, rather than blast out; to keep ourselves quietly and in a contained way when we traverse into nature, with respect, and an awareness that *this is real* – not a cartoon – and so shift seamlessly from our lives into the wild, and back again, without spoiling or disrupting or destroying. Although newt holds other symbolism, it's the eye of this primordial creature which interests me, and which is cited in that famous incantation by the three witches in *Macbeth*. They include eye of newt because it contains a specific kind of magic, and that's the magic of sight and seeing; of viewing the world as an animal in it, rather than a separate, god-like master above and beyond.

I'm a creature of pop culture, as you will have guessed already – putting modern and ancient, popular and timeless, together is part of my calling! – and 'Newt' is the name of the little, lone girl who survives the onslaught of terrible creatures in the film *Aliens*. She learns to see like an alien in this narrative. Her newt's eye allows her to do this. We can meditate (magick, for some of you) and bring that eye into our aura; ask for it to become our own. Mediation and magick is the 'quicker way' of achieving change and self-transformation, sometimes, but also my own experience has been that very often the greater, more powerful magick has been to act (or not act) in the physical realm. I think that moving away from screen images of the natural world and going for walks and hikes, swims and cycles, in it, allows us to experience and feel the wonder of nature as a documentary, film, or cartoon cannot do. The newt's slow-slow-quick pace might, also, be one we can emulate, because it is that slow langouring in the wild which allows us to note her marvels: the colours and textures of leaves; the slow hum and flit of tiny insects and flies; the light dappling and dancing as birds sing from their secret, leaf-cloaked places.

But then, we can also be quick, moving on so as not to scare or disturb; adopting a nomadic, newt-like swiftness but slowing, then, to re-train our eye so that it becomes the newt's green one, rather than our usual, greedy, 'what can I get' one. The heart of the green movement is one which puts green dollars lower down on an imaginary list, and the green of nature at the very top of it. Our eye must transmute if we are to accomplish this in a real and lasting way. And, once it begins to shift, it's easy to 'see' how beautiful, bountiful, and wonderful the natural world is – a world which isn't separate from our own, but is one with it. The aim of eco-spirituality is to show us the ways and means of shifting towards this deep understanding – this knowing – which is the aim of mysticism or magic – whichever path you find yourself on – and which is also the aim of this slim but intentionally written little book.

Chapter 8

Wool of bat

There's a joke – I forget how it goes – but the humour lies around the idea of 'bat milk' – the bat as an animal we can 'milk'. Ridiculous, right? Although, the funny thing about this joke, so to speak, is that it's based on the truism that we human beings try to consume *everything*. I must include myself as part of this generalism. I am a person who, alongside their inclinations of the spirit, was also born into a body that is very sensual, sensory, sense-based. I love music and perfume, clothes and food. I feel as if I've always harboured a desire to eat the world – I love eating, probably more than any other of life's joys (and I enjoy all of them to a very great extent indeed!).

Related to this is the fact that I have always possessed an entrepreneurial way of looking at things. This mode is borne of my working class background, perhaps; it is aligned to that most compelling literary narrative form, the 'rags to riches' tale, or *bildungsroman*. This 'hero's journey' sees the protagonist move from nothing to something; from a place of want, need, and poverty, perhaps as a peasant, orphan, or outcast, to the position of lord, gentleman, or king. Perhaps, in some true life tales, he 'makes it' as a celebrity or sportsman. Or perhaps she becomes a supermodel or a world famous writer. I've veered, in my thinking and inclinations, all my life, between a part of me that sees the world as a vehicle for transformation, and a part of me that sees the world as an endless source of opportunity. I have no doubt I could have been an entrepreneur, and have run many little money-making ventures alongside my writing in order to sustain it. I keenly understand and empathise with those who look at the world and see a chance to turn what it freely provides into money, which is the medium we need to buy food and shelter. This is the basis of capitalism, and it's the mechanism in which our lives and culture sit. It's a human quality, to want to provide for ourselves; to obtain not just the essentials but also a better quality of life; and I don't think we should necessary rate this as 'bad', in and of itself. I see it as part of our survival instinct, and it can result in great creative outputs as well as be a real force for good, too.

Essentially, the entrepreneur spins straw into gold. It's the stuff of fairytales. Except, instead of pulling a silver dress out of a nut, or finding a key to the kingdom in the stomach of a fish, what's usually found or filched are the simple raw materials supplied by the Earth's body. Of necessity, what's also created are the toil and tears of less fortunate human beings. We can only create palaces and robes, carriages and feasts, by chopping down trees, clearing vast tracts of land, churning up stones and metals, foraging for fuels, and having some people employed in jobs that are minimum wage, or less in many places around the world, to keep the whole system going and life generally comfortable or even luxurious for those who are higher up in the echelons of this prince-peasant hierarchy.

Then, there are the waste products not included within this miraculous narrative – the leftovers, the unusable, the rubbish. When we think of waste, we think of the petrochemical industry, the oil industry, the motor industry; but almost every type of industry creates waste, from these ones you can easily imagine, to those creating clothing and materials, to those dealing with water, energy, and agriculture. In fact, waste is as abundant as the abundance created by industry itself: the creation of clothing, of food, of products like paper and printing ink, of everyday items, of the energy we need and use from moment to moment, creates it. When you look at lists of these waste materials and substances, it's clear that we're squatting over and fouling upon the Earth continuously, and it follows that our faecal matter is too plentiful for the Earth to transmogrify, and some of it is too unsavoury for the Earth to ingest / digest at all. Think radioactive waste; pesticide waste; biological waste; asbestos waste; acid and alkaline waste; and so many more besides. (Nemerow and Agardy, 1998)

We use the term 'bat shit' to intimate that someone or something is 'crazy', but how crazy is this? Not only are we milking the Earth – have milked it – for everything it's got, and even beyond the threshold of possible replenishment in some cases: we've also created waste – poisons and pollutions – which have in turn upset and upended the Earth's natural self-cleansing processes, putting them entirely out of whack. We would, in theory, take the milk of the bat, if we could; and the wool of a bat, if that was possible (never mind that 'wool of bat' was, in the three witches' incantation, possibly a folk name for holly leaves – which shouldn't be ingested, by the way, as they are mildly toxic to humans). Never mind that bats are now, thanks to us, endangered: whales are, too, but still we eat them; tigers and lions are, but still we hunt them; insects are on the wane, dropping dead in fields in droves, but still we spray them with chemicals and pesticides, because having veg that looks nice is more important their tiny souls and the continuation of their entire line. We arrow birds from the air, and hook fish from the sea, whether for food, or sport, or because we think them 'pests'. Even though the planet needs us not to; even though our trapping and killing of animals is trapping and killing us as well. How batty, how bat shit, is that?

Witches, it's reputed, could transform themselves into bats. Women, over time, transmute into them, too, becoming 'old bats', that is, sour and opinionated older women, who are a little bit crazy, a little bit evil and spooky, as well, perhaps. This is that same cultural vision, which is aligned with the male gaze, that we've looked at in previous chapters. The old woman as mad and not worth listening to. The old woman as cray-cray; nuts-o; bats. As I get older, I want to inhibit my voice, my views, less and less; but there's the risk, then, in this culture of moving from 'tongue of dog' out to 'old bat' that I will become an archetypal 'grumpy old woman', who is viewed as negative and nasty simply for giving her personal opinions. A bat emits high-pitched squeaks and squeals, and we are encouraged to 'hear' the voice of any old woman similarly, and not to pay it any mind. The voices of older women, in our society, grow higher and higher until, eventually, they are out of our hearing range, their pitch entirely beyond the capabilities of our cultural ears.

As our population grows, there are more and more old women, however. Mature women. Wise women, even. I don't personally believe that age in and of itself equates to wisdom, but by the sheer fact of having lived on this Earth for a longer time than ourselves, an older woman holds knowledge and insight which could prove invaluable and are worth listening to. True, she may hold prejudices too, especially as we shift beyond the restrictive, reactive 'isms' of many previous generations into a more enlightened way of thinking; but does this mean she should be told to pipe down? Older people deserve their voice and their views as much as anyone else, and there is no reason why a man should grow to become 'an elder statesman' and an older woman should degenerate into 'an old bat', except that, in our culture, "women are linked to... inferior qualities of nature, just as men are associated with the superior qualities of reason and intellect" (Blackie, 2019).

Old woman Earth's voice has also been cruelly ignored. She's been shrieking for decades, if not a couple of hundred years; the sound was barely a whisper, once, but now it's cut right through the fog of ignorance; penetrated the wall of indifference; and all of us can definitely hear it. We know what we are doing to the body of our old mother, as her veins grow sluggish with sewage, and her water tables are laden with pollution, and her wide, bright seas stuffed with a steady stew of vomited scrap, crap, and plastic. We've pilfered and filched – taken more than we should have – and in return for her generosity and bounty have buried our rubbish heaps in her flesh, poured sluice and hazardous waste down her throat, and made some areas of her body not just unsightly and ugly but dangerous and deadly, toxic and uninhabitable. If we incinerate our waste, then these emissions may carry 'persistent pollutants' such as dioxins, furans, metals and mercury that can affect not only those living close to the facility but "can be carried long distances from their emission sources, go through various chemical and physical transformations, and pass numerous times through soil, water, or food" (Waste incineration & public health, 2000). If we bury it, then "it can contaminate the earth, and could cause infection or diseases" (Gay, 2015), not just if the landfill site is improperly managed, but because this is the nature of waste, particularly waste which is protected by earth and layers of further waste from the oxygen and water that assist bacteria in the process of decomposition.

Plastic and glass may take millions of years to decompose, if at all, in any case. And now microplastics are an issue, too, making their way, along with packaging and other macroplastics, into the bellies and bodies of sea-dwelling creatures, from whales and fish to mussels and shrimps, down to lungworms and even sea plankton. Although we're still looking into the effect of this form of waste pollution, "It is likely that there are… a range of sub-lethal effects that have not yet been recognised" (Harrison and Hester, 2018).

Needless to say, we're doing something crazy, once again, and as old woman Earth cries out, can we really keep believing that *she* is 'bats' and *we* are sane? That her female voice is still to be ignored? These issues affect us, harm us, and we have now entered the first phase of an extinction level event – "The current rate of extinction is between 100 and 1,000 times higher than the pre-human background rate of extinction, which is jaw-dropping. We are definitely going through a sixth mass extinction" (What is mass extinction and are we facing a sixth one?, 2022). How batshit is it, that we create materials that are almost immortal, whilst on the verge of wiping ourselves out…?

We have taken and taken, too much. Consider the body of the bat – yes, we have taken, and used, almost every part of it, as just one small example of how we take – take – take. Its meat, of course, is eaten. Its blood has been – and still is – used as a folk medicine. Its bones have been used to make spears, and its teeth have been / are used as jewellery; once, like the eels of British rivers, they were even used as currency. And 'wool of bat' – yes, this too, has in fact been harvested by healers for certain purposes, and the bat's skin has been dried and used by certain peoples at certain times to make, for example, items of entertainment such as kites.

But our resourcefulness is rendering us resource-less. These creatures are now in peril, and "many bat species around the world are vulnerable or endangered due to factors ranging from loss and fragmentation of habitat, diminished food supply, destruction of roosts, disease and hunting or killing of bats" (Threats to bats - About Bats - Bat Conservation Trust, 2022). Many other animals are in trouble, too, of course, and many flora and fauna that feed us are running out, from tuna fish to bananas and cocoa. Soil itself is becoming 'endangered', and water also, as climate change takes hold, and these essentials become more and more an expensive 'commodity'. Famines and droughts are predicted for many parts of the world in the near future, and the food crisis is running towards us, hand-in-hand with the climate crisis.

According to the Wildfowl and Wetlands Trust, a British bat eats up to 3,000 insects in a single night, with a pursuit / capture rate of up to two per second. Insects are also becoming fewer and fewer, too, however. The seemingly erratic flight path of bats is because they need to swoop and dive, echolocating this huge number of insect prey and moving quickly to catch it.

If we want to survive, we need to emulate the bat's swiftness and ability to change paths as needed. We think to become more agile, more flexible, and think not of our wants but our needs. The bat needs to eat 3,000 tiny insects – do we need to eat so much meat ourselves? Cattle farming is one of primary causes of deforestation and desertification in the world. Do we need to consume so much at all, in fact? We must work to transform ourselves, deliberately, into bats, in this sense, and swoop not just to new and daring conclusions, but to new and daring actions as well. Talk is cheap, and we've done so much of it – our squeaking, as the world begins to burn, is becoming meaningless, and soon we won't be able to hear ourselves whining – or shrieking – above the crackle of the flames.

Chapter 9

Howlet's wing

The wetlands opened my eyes, as I squinted into their gloom, to the beauty of 'dark creatures': creatures that are dark in colour; the animals of mud and bog; critters that exist in hollows, like slow worms, or else come alive in the darkness of night, like bats.

Probably the most beautiful nocturnal creature in the UK is the owl. Returning to childhood favourite – the film *Labyrinth* – of course David Bowie's goblin king had the ability to transform himself into a beautiful snowy owl. No man could be shown turning into a bat, and retain any kind of grandiosity – bats are for witches, or else, if men, then they must be vampires. Maybe vampires can be cool, but they're a little bit passé, perhaps, and they are slinky, skinny, slightly creepy creatures, generally. An owl is more majestic in our cultural thinking than a bat, as are its associations, of wisdom, knowledge, scholarliness, etc. Bats and owls abound in wetlands areas and, despite differences in our perception, both, as animals of the air, hold a special place in our imaginations and, if we are so inclined, in our magical thinking and in our magical practices, too. The owl is a witch's messenger, after all; in older tales, witches can transform into them, and they are not exclusive to men as they seem to have become in our contemporary cultural thinking.

Although the Hindu 'vaha' – animal deities, and usually the mounts of those gods and goddesses who are in more human-like form – are supposedly entirely male, my own encounter with the owl-headed 'god' of this pantheon was very interesting. I received an undeniable impression of them as female. I'd be very interested in hearing of others' encounters with Uluka / Ulooka and what they sensed in that case. I think making a rule of 'all male' doesn't make logical sense unless you personally encounter the deities yourself and can check this out. My impression, as I say, was of an intelligent, deep, and calm being, full of wisdom – and, also, that she is a being brimming with feminine energy. Being wise and being a woman were naturally combined in that owl deity, and it was a sweet surprise for me when I discovered this.

When we think of owls in this culture, they are nearly always male. One exception was mythical Greek princess Nyctimene who, after being raped by her father, was transformed into an owl by the goddess Athena (in the Roman version of this tale, this transfiguration is performed by Minerva), and made into her familiar. The owl became, over time, the symbol of Athena; Minerva, of course, carries one, too. Both were virgin goddesses, yet both have this 'vaha' (riding on their shoulders, however, rather than they on her's), this familiar, at their side. Whilst this origin of the owl isn't in all stories, this particular possibility speaks powerfully to me, as a survivor of similar abuse. I don't think we can so easily say that this trauma is transmuted into wisdom – I think this then transmutes the trauma, too, by making its 'outcome' positive. My personal belief is that the abuse, including the rape, of children, is the greatest evil on this planet, and those who perpetrate it are the 'vaha' of Evil. I agree with the late fantasy writer Terry Pratchett's definition of evil, that it is the reduction of living things – whether animal, vegetable, or mineral – to objects. To reduce the living body of a child to an object that is used to scratch a sexual urge is monstrous.

The philosopher Emmanuel Kant is responsible for much of our cultural thinking on objectivity. In his words: "sexual love makes of the loved person an Object of appetite; as soon as that appetite has been stilled, the person is cast aside as one casts away a lemon which has been sucked dry. ... as soon as a person becomes an Object of appetite for another, all motives of moral relationship cease to function, because as an Object of appetite for another a person becomes a thing and can be treated and used as such by everyone" (Kant Lectures on Ethics, 163). Although Kant was clear that both men and women may be objectified, he also stated that this was far more likely to happen to women. Our culture has evolved to normalise this objectification of half its human inhabitants, essentially.

Objectification is also a central tenet in feminist theory, particularly as it relates to the body as a sexual object. "Martha Nussbaum has listed seven features inherent within this idea:

1. *instrumentality*: the treatment of a person as a tool for the objectifier's purposes;
2. *denial of autonomy*: the treatment of a person as lacking in autonomy and self-determination;
3. *inertness*: the treatment of a person as lacking in agency, and perhaps also in activity;
4. *fungibility*: the treatment of a person as interchangeable with other objects;
5. *violability*: the treatment of a person as lacking in boundary-integrity;
6. *ownership*: the treatment of a person as something that is owned by another (can be bought or sold);
7. *denial of subjectivity*: the treatment of a person as something whose experiences and feelings (if any) need not be taken into account.

Rae Langton has added three more features to Nussbaum's list:

8. *reduction to body*: the treatment of a person as identified with their body, or body parts;
9. *reduction to appearance*: the treatment of a person primarily in terms of how they look, or how they appear to the senses;

10.*silencing*: the treatment of a person as if they are silent, lacking the capacity to speak." (Papadaki, 2019)

My own experience of being used as an object – a sexual object, by my father – resulted in trauma. I suffered from many strange and distressing thoughts about myself as a young person as a result. One was that I was, somehow, made of dirt. This was compounded by my mother telling me that my skin was dirty on the upper inside of my thighs; really, I just had slightly darker skin in that area, which is normal – but my mother, not knowing this, told me around the age of 10 or 11 that it was 'ingrained dirt', and I should try to clean it off. Needless to say, this wasn't possible to remove, but I still spent many years trying to fulfil this command, sometimes scrubbing myself until I bled, or even attempting to take the skin completely away, because that seemed like a 'logical' way of removing the 'dirt' for good. It took a very long time, and much self-work, to realise that this was nonsense; also to realise that what happened to me at the hands of my father had compounded the issue, causing me to truly believe that my body – and my body as a sexual object in particular – was dirty, muddy, stinky and filthy.

When I came to the wetlands, I had done a lot of work on myself with regards to this. I didn't believe I was made of dirt anymore. I was initially attracted to the wetlands by their beauty, not by their dirt. But there is a saying, that the most beautiful blooms grow from the filthiest mud. This is true of the gorgeous plants found in bogs and fens. We, as victims of abuse, can try to emulate these plants by attempting to grow from that initial place of darkness and dirt – the dirt, not of ourselves, but put onto us by the 'dirty', depraved actions of another – and endeavouring to become who we were meant to be – the best and brightest possible version of ourselves.

However, I would not like to paint any child abuser as a kind of 'gardener', which would be the temptation for such a person within this analogy – what an abuser does is selfish, degrading, damaging, and hugely, wholly wrong. It irrevocably hurts the body of the child along with their mind, emotions, and soul so fully and with such violent force that many victims never recover enough, even over the course of a lifetime, to fulfil even a fraction of their innate potential. Survival alone can be the only 'outcome' in many cases and for some victims, of course, there is not even this. Existence is too terribly painful for some that they seek to end their own lives. For much of my early life, I felt this way myself, and did, in my late twenties, make a plan to kill myself. Luckily, for just one reason – I couldn't bear to think of anyone seeing the chaos of my living conditions after I'd gone! – I didn't do this; and, soon after that, poetry swooped in, and I began in earnest on a suitable spiritual path after not, previously, finding any that I has gelled with.

I then, for a time, enjoyed being a performer, reading out my poems on not just poetry but comedy and cabaret circuits, and having what felt like my teenage years rather later than most – the abuse had stunted me, in many ways, so that I had stopped moving and progressing emotionally and experientially at a young age. This 'freezing' of self I think is typical and, although there are few studies looking at this sort of 'age regression', it's a commonly held belief by therapists that trauma may cause it; certainly, abuse at a young age does impede normal brain development, it's been found, leading to "a host of biopsychosocial domains including: earlier onsets of puberty, cognitive deficits, depression, dissociative symptoms, maladaptive sexual development, hypothalamic–pituitary–adrenal attenuation, asymmetrical stress responses, high rates of obesity, more major illnesses and healthcare utilization, dropping out of high school, persistent posttraumatic stress disorder, self-mutilation, *Diagnostic and Statistical Manual of Mental Disorders* diagnoses, physical and sexual revictimization, premature deliveries, teen motherhood, drug and alcohol abuse, and domestic violence" (Trickett et al., 2011).

I find it painful and pertinent that Athena / Minerva's advisor is this creature potentially signifying rape / incest / child abuse. The owl, in this case, is a symbol of the survivor, and the 'wisdom' which comes from that, not because of what happened, but in spite of it. This ghostly creature represents the spirit that continues on and even flies free of the body when it is immobilised by fear and the terrible torture of rape. Minerva's feathered friend is often depicted specifically as a little owl, which is the smallest of the owl species, as if to inmate both the fact that sexual abuse may have happened when we were very young, and that this 'small voice' – of a child; of our inner child, then – should be listened to. When we make great decisions, the voices of the smallest, and the least powerful, should be heeded; in fact, they should be the powerful's greatest advisor. The word 'minister' comes from the Old French *ministre* and, in turn, the Latin *minister*, meaning 'servant'. I've long felt that ministers and politicians should relearn this and re-root in this – their role, in my eyes, is not to 'lead', as a single ego, but to act in service to the many. Although this idealist stance comes up against some issues when we take into account, for example, ingrained prejudices, mob mentality, and lack of education for large swathes of people, the principle remains, I feel. The ideal must be tempered to fit reality, but it should never be forgotten.

The owl – the howlet – symbolises this ability of survivors to rise above the terrible 'dirt' put upon them by abusers – the shame, guilt, and serious emotional and mental ravages that are suffered. I think, although we can try to be like the flowers, and 'bloom', very often we must simply 'take wing', forgetting the dirt, and the sad sense that grey, gruel-like bogs can reinforce, lifting ourselves up by our own innate willpower. For me, this taking wing took place literally during episodes of abuse, when I dissociated from my body and found my own spirit standing outside of it, looking on. The pain and shock of what was happening was too much for me, and this was the only way my mind and soul could survive. I took wing, too, by repressing and forgetting these incidents as much as I could, smothering most of my early childhood within a kind of mental fog. Later, the 'taking wing' took place in a less dramatic but no less imperative way, as I turned to poetry and spirituality as a means of salving my wounds. Poetry gave me self-expression and the emotional means of investigating into and understanding what had happened. It provided a powerful outlet – writing – whilst I remembered and recollected what has happened. My spiritual studies allowed me to realise how those events had shaped and stunted me and, with assistance – of humans, angels, ancestors, and other entities, includes the gods – to heal myself as best I could.

We survivors may just be little owls, with little voices, but we possess an experiential understanding of how some can be cruel, and others can be kind. The beautiful heart-shaped face of the snowy owl is a fantastic reminder of this, even as its killing claws pierce and tear its prey. A survivor isn't a saint – if I look at myself, at my personality, then, because of that trauma, it is soft and vulnerable in some places, and hard and defensive in others. It's perhaps underdeveloped or stunted in certain spots, and overdeveloped and worldly in others. This unwieldy mix can result in awkwardness, abruptness, inappropriateness, I have found. In his book, *Soul Murder,* Leonard Shengold writes about the trauma of sexual abuse and how it can cause a child to develop "defensive psychological measures against feeling"; of the confusion and complexity that results, so that victims "often cannot properly register what they want and how they feel"; and generally of the "devastated psychic structure" caused by the rape / seduction of a child (whether forced or enticed, sexual acts performance by an adult on a child are classified as abuse). The child, of course, still craves care, still needs love, still loves their parent, even if that parent is the abuser; and so there's that tormenting mix in there, too, as the child is hurt, damaged, ravaged, defiled, but given basic care, even fed with titbits of affection, perhaps – like a magnificent wild bird that is kept in cage and offered only scraps.

But Shengold writes too about those who 'survive', and about the mental strength that is required to do so without perpetuating cycles of abuse – for example, on one's own children – or falling prey to more serious mental ill health or issues of addiction. Not everyone does survive to this degree or even at all, of course, and the women I personally know who have managed to become respectable human beings also suffer from issues such as poor self-image, chronic lack of confidence, depression and despondency, disassociation, high levels of stress and distress, bouts of more serious mental illness, and other things besides. Still, owls are symbols of death, and of transformation. They emerge from the darkness into the light. They live within the dark, seeing clearly. My own experience, beyond these issues of mind and emotion, are that, like the owl, we can emerge from darkness into light – can even learn to see into that darkness – and we do this by finding our true self – the light within – and connecting to it.

I have found the wetlands to be a murky mirror to my survivor self. In this case, projection is personal, not cultural; temporary, not fixed; and is a means of profound self-understanding. Murky, sludgy pools become vagina-like in this analogy. If this terrain is a person, then she is a woman, but less an eerie water nymph than a kind of bog woman, or even a bog witch. The magic she – I – must perform is that of transmuting her own view of her body – from dirty, grubby, and polluted, to rich, fertile, even beautiful. We can begin by noting that mud leads to gorgeous outcomes, such as flowers; and that, even when there is no such conclusion, mud is necessary. We can thus accept the mud of our own bodies as vital, and important. There is wisdom in the body, and we have to keep listening in order to begin hearing it. So many times I've listened out in the dark, yearning to hear the call of an owl, hoping to see that howlet's wing brightening the darkness, a flash of silver shooting through the gloom, and we have to be just as alert to the messages of the body itself. The energy bodies are aligned with the physical body, for sure, so I have found that this listening has led not just to a greater sense of what my physical body needs, but has acted as a gateway to the spiritual – to the chakras, the meridians, and the various layers of self. The sludgy body is therefore a magick portal, in a sense, and if we give it our ear then it will whisper its secrets, its knowledge, its wisdom, as clearly as an owl cry in the stillness of the night. And it will offer up, if we remain alert, that pale ghostly aspect of ourselves, so that we learn not just of the physical self / realm, but the realms within and beyond – the spirit, our soul, which sits in the still forest within us, waiting to take flight.

Chapter 10

Hell-broth

If the wetlands are a cauldron, then we have thought of them as full of 'hell-broth' – dirt, ooze, and unkempt chaos which we have attempted to 'civilise' through land reclamation and development. The murky soup of a foggy day tempts us towards this thinking: the gruel-like earth sucking our boots into the wetland sludge; the strange, dun-coloured plant life squatting over dangerously hidden pools; the midges and mozzies biting our faces as we are itched by hordes of nettles and brambles. Frogs thrust their spear-heads up out of the water to dolefully stare whilst dragonfly larvae writhe fatly in the ooze. The names of the plants, here, are very different to roses, lilies, and tulips; in fact, they are more brazen, more brutish, and we could well imagine that these are the flowers of a more hellish place: bogbean; pillwort; brooklime; loosestrife; lesser spearwort; common water-crowfoot; spiked water-milfoil; rigid hornwort. No easy images come to mind when we learn these names; there are no poems or songs about such. They spike the tongue as they spike us underfoot; they sound more like the true names of demons that of innocent flora; and what they intimate, in their unfamiliarity and association, is danger.

In the UK, there is very little danger, of course. Other wetlands might harbour crocs or snakes, but we have none of the former and the latter are exceedingly rare. We simply project a hellish sense onto these misunderstood places, and this has been, in the end, to our own detriment. Thinking that they are full of devils, whether they are supernatural monsters, watery wastes, or weeds, we have hacked and hunted the wetlands into submission. A review in 2014 stated that, on a global scale, "the reported long-term loss of natural wetlands averages between

54–57% but loss may have been as high as 87% since 1700 AD" (Davidson, 2014). And these are only the reported losses. "Across the U.S. and Canada, the vast majority of wetlands — about 85 percent — have been destroyed in the name of agricultural expansion" (*Wetlands Update — Has Preservation Had an Impact?*, 2022). In the UK, "we've lost 90% of our wetland habitats in the last 100 years" (Water | The Wildlife Trusts, 2022), too – wetlands, being seen as wastelands, have been consistently, relentlessly decimated.

Here in Wales, within my own memory, Cardiff wetlands has been flooded and then 'reinstated' elsewhere – needless to say, this did involve the loss of wildlife as well as important habitats; the Gwent Levels have been under threat from the potential creation of a new, high-speed byroad; Kenfig National Nature Reserve, which includes slow-to-grow and incredibly delicate sand dunes alongside a large wetland area, has struggled to find new lease owners – among its many flora and fauna are rarities such as the fen orchid, medicinal leech, petalwort, great crested newt, hairy dragonfly, and great bittern, a bird I recently saw fly and was perhaps the most unusual bark-like shard of avian aerial magic I've ever witnessed. And these are only those wetlands within a short distance of my home. Since Wales possesses coast along three of its edges, there are many, many wetland areas, and there have been – and are – many, many instances in which they have been / are still endangered.

As we have seen, though, the benefits of wetlands are many:

Water Cleansing

Wetlands are often called the planet's kidneys, as they effectively filter our water supply. They can "remove up to 60% of metals in water and eliminate up to 90% or nitrogen, purifying it so life can thrive" (Why wetlands, 2022). Other studies have found that wetlands remove pollutants at a rate that would cost millions annually if undertaken by a waste water treatment plant. Some wetlands replenish groundwater, which is a common source of drinking water for humans; many are capable of removing nitrogen and phosphorous from surface water, too. Since just 1% of the Earth's water is accessible by humans, then this makes the work of wetlands even more vital.

Carbon Holding

Wetlands store carbon in both their live plant biomass as well as preserved (peat) biomass. Here, it is effectively kept from being released into the atmosphere as carbon dioxide, which is a well-known greenhouse gas that is contributing to climate change.

Erosion Control

Wetlands provide erosion control that is important for maintaining our coastlines and combatting the ever increasing danger of coastal erosion. Already in Wales we have made a decision recently to allow one of our coastal villages – Fairbourne – to simply slide into the sea – the cost of reclamation is too much. We cannot fight the ocean on our own – nature, through wetlands, does a much better job of defending against it, and always has.

Flood Protection

Wetlands are natural sponges, soaking up water and holding it there before releasing it incrementally over time. In this way, surface water, rain water, ground water, flood water and, in some areas, snowmelt, are slowed and more evenly distributed. This process allows time for water to infiltrate into the ground. Trees, tree roots, and other wetland vegetation also act as a stopper and slower of potential flooding.

Biodiversity

Wetlands are as rich as rainforests in their biodiversity, providing a home to an incredible number of flora and fauna. "Coral reefs and mangroves are some of the most biodiverse habitats in the world and freshwater wetlands host more species per square kilometre than land or oceans including one third of all vertebrate species" (What is biodiversity and why do we need it?, 2022). The Wildfowl & Wetlands Trust (WWT) call them 'super systems' for their sheer, extraordinary level of biodiversity.

Additionally, wetland areas are "biological supermarkets" (Why are Wetlands Important? | US EPA, 2022). They are home to huge numbers of not just flora and fauna – reptiles, birds, fish, mammals, and insects – but also microbes and particles of organic material that are made from broken down plants stems and leaves. This 'detritus', as it's known, then becomes food for small fish and insects, which then, in turn, becomes food for larger animals living within the wetland ecosystem. Returning to the image of the howlet, then – although her white wings are what we envisage when we think of a spooky wetland, beneath these exist a complex ecosystem of species inter-dependency. Wetlands lead to microbes, lead to insects, lead to food for the howlet's hungry beak, and for the mouths of snakes, frogs, bats, and myriad other animals. Although all wetlands are different, within each of them sits a complicated and fragile web of this sort. If we see even one element within this as a 'pest' and attempt to remove it, in reality we are eradicating other plants and creatures, too.

We know, now, that bogs are not hellish places, but by their removal we have caused a "hell-broth" of a different sort, via our unwieldy, unyielding, unthinking urbanisation of everything. Our 'solution' to muck and mud has been to slather it with concrete – to bury all that green goodness alive. Because of our grabbing, our incessant greed, wetlands are almost constantly in danger, from the twin threats of land development and coastal erosion. Inland wetlands have been reduced by 87% worldwide since the beginning of the last century. The 'hell-broth' is therefore not the sticky, icky, oozy wetlands which, to a prospector's eye, seem to be mostly mud – it's the chaos we create when we interrupt and upturn nature. So many rare species are here, from natterjack toads to king beetles, wild peonies to otters and adders. They are vital to our survival; as vital as rainforests are to the overall wellbeing of the Earth.

Currently, there are cranes and diggers all over the city of Cardiff, which is the fastest growing city in Europe, edging ever closer to the wetlands, which has already been once relocated. The toads and beetles sit blinking, slow-breathing, their little hearts and lungs unaware of this threat; the adder's tongue forks in the bracken, not knowing that it is in danger of being silenced; the howlet continues to take wing, into the dark – and into a future that may not include it as a species at all. We have not mentioned the 'lizard's leg' of the witches' chant, but in one energy work session with a friend, we saw her ambition take the form, in our mind's eye, of a lizard – languid, lazy, conniving, calculating, and capable, when compelled, of furious speed. It reminded me at once of a poem by Rebecca Tamás called *spell for reptiles: "behind a black eye / the comfort of venom" (Tamás, 2019)*. Our ambition sits and stares, jerking into action when it sees something it wants – like the tongue of a reptile, flicking out to hook in a fat and juicy fly. We pay no mind to the fly, it exists only to feed us, and we swallow it down like a sweet, without even chewing; our consumption of the natural world has been the same, and so the entire earth is under threat.

We must make a change, inward and outward, and we must make it now, if it – and we – are to survive.

I walk. The path takes me from a thin river, to a widening plain, eventually out to the sea's blue-grey expanse. At my right, the river's banks are invariably muddy, mucky, and mulchy. But the gloop is dark and rich, packed thick with obvious fertility. And in places this chocolate brown blooms into bright, broccoli green, the stacked heaps and slicks of mud spurting into rounded mounds of soft, mossy grass; into tall, golden swathes of feathering reeds. There's a rich, distinct land here – the wet-land – and I catch sight of its inhabitants as I walk: a lone, silver heron, still as a coin in a purse; the crimson flash of redshanks, which feed and breed here, their long legs the colour of a postbox; a V of geese who arrow through air to the water's edge, skimming to stillness, their long necks trumpeting as they land.

The birds are here because the marshland provides them with food, as well as a place to rest or nest. The water and mud provide plentiful opportunities for them. The opportunities they present for us have been outlined in this book, I hope. They are a very vital part of the world's magick and, where I live, of the magic of Britain itself. As nature words slip out and away, banished from our modern dictionaries, and species of flora and fauna become extinct on a daily basis, it's by the river, beside the estuary, on the mud bank that we can re-learn what's important, even when overlooking the wetland rather than stepping into it.

The Magic of Britain
Inspired by 'the lost words' recently removed from the Children's Oxford Dictionary

The magic of Britain is failing, is fading
Arthur is sleeping and Merlin's no more
No sowing or growing, just moaning, bewailing
As precious plants die and birds fall to the floor

I sing you a world that is now close to ending
Of lapwings and skylarks and frogspawn and hawks
As spiders entwine what is theirs in the shading
And sunshine inspires us from dusk until dawn

I tell you the magic of Britain is fading
The lost words we once knew are nearly forgotten
The cuckoo is quiet in the once-dappled glading
The thrush has gone hush and the acorn is rotten

Moss has been lost and the beech has been breached
The bluebell's been plucked and the mistletoe's missing
Cowslip and conker have slipped from our speech
The newt is now mute and the ivy's stopped kissing

Because - the magic of Britain is fading
No more is the adder that added its tongue
To the song of the forest, the woodland is failing
The willow is weeping, the ash has gone dumb

The cuckoo is silent, the nightingale's song
Is rare, because where it was everything's changing
The once-world of Arthur and Merlin is gone
The magic, the magic of Britain is fading

Eventually, I leave the wetlands, returning to the city which is, very often, not far away, its edges germ-ing ever closer to the water. The blare of sirens, roar of cars, and heavy, held-in sense that comes from so much enclosing, encircling concrete – both underfoot and overhead – combine to make this truly an 'urban jungle'; the mish-mash of roads and roundabouts, the mix of blockish buildings in a thousand different styles, the stressing bodies of too-many-people, creating a chaotic, cantankerous crush. Gone are the golden feather grass and silvering birds, their songs soft on the bright Welsh breeze; instead is a meld of everything man-made; of everything not-nature. It's as if Ceridwen's cauldron has been tipped upside down, with the morals, here, holding consumption at their heart instead of connection. The contents of the city spill out unchecked, combining convenience with crime, culture with a cut-off from community. It is an unfulfilling soup; an unsatisfying concoction. In its showiness and splendour, its emptiness and ugliness, it is a kind of hell-broth, offering sugar with one hand, isolation and misery with the other.

Let's stop projecting this darkness – this hellishness – which is of our own making – onto wetlands, painting them as a wasteland. They clearly are not, and our repression and repugnance have yielded only sorrow and sadness for ourselves, in the end, with the loss of countless species; the near-death and endangerment of others; disconnect and distress for ourselves. Let us remember that green is good, that blue is vital, but that brown is important, too. Nature wears this as just one of her colours, and it is time, now, for Nature to rise, in all of her many forms and guises, as the river goddess; the forest goddess; the sea goddess; the goddess of the mountains. And as the bog goddess, too – murky and muddy, fetid and fulsome and fierce. Her body, and our body, are one. Her heart, and ours, are the same. The fire breath of life that glows inside a toad, inside a newt, inside an adder, inside an owl, burns in us as well. And it – and she – are – and always will be – sacred. The bog witch, and the witches of the other terrains, know it. And now you know it, too.

Notes

2000. *Waste incineration & public health*. Washington, D.C.: National Academy Press, p.4.

2022. *Threats to bats - About Bats - Bat Conservation Trust*. [online] Bat Conservation Trust. Available at: https://www.bats.org. uk/about-bats/threats-to-bats

Blackie, S., 2019. *If Women Rose Rooted*, Tewkesbury, Gloucestershire: September Publishing, p.33.

Boyce, J., 2021. in *Imperial mud: The fight for the fens*. London: Icon Books, p. 24.

Cixous, H., Sellers, S. and Derrida, J. 2004. *The Hélène Cixous Reader*. London: Routledge.

The Countryside Code: Advice for Countryside Visitors. GOV.UK. Available at: https://www.gov.uk/government/publications/ the-countryside-code/the-countryside-code-advice-for-countryside-visitors.

Davidson, N., 2014. How much wetland has the world lost? Long-term and recent trends in global wetland area. *Marine and Freshwater Research*, 65(10), p.934.

Department for Work and Pensions, 2019. Households Below Average Income (HBAI) Quality and Methodology Information Report. London: UK Government.

Duffin, Christopher., 2010. The Toad Stone – a rather unlikely gem. Jewellery History Today. 3-4.

Gibson, D., 1996. Broken Down By Age And Gender. Gender & Society, 10(4), pp.433-448.

Halliday, W., 1921. *Snake stones*. London: David Nutt, for the Folk-Lore Society, p.118.

Harrison, R. and Hester, R., 2018. *Plastics and the environment*. Royal Society of Chemistry, p.73.

Kant, I., Heath, P. and Schneewind, J.B., 2001. *Lectures on ethics*. Cambridge, U.K.: Cambridge University Press.

Lee, Y., 2019. The Toad Houses as a Symbol of Transformation of Maternity. *Journal of Symbols & Sandplay Therapy*, 10(2), p.27-28.

Markson, E. and Hess, B., 1980. Older Women in the City. *Signs: Journal of Women in Culture and Society*, 5(S3), pp. S127-S142.

Maund, P., Irvine, K., Reeves, J., Strong, E., Cromie, R., Dallimer, M. and Davies, Z., 2019. Wetlands for Wellbeing: Piloting a Nature-Based Health Intervention for the Management of Anxiety and Depression. *International Journal of Environmental Research and Public Health*, 16(22), p.4413.

McConnell, G., 2018. "Worm", *PN Review 239*, 44(3).

Millman, O., 2022. *Anthropomorphism: how much humans and animals share is still contested*. [online] the Guardian. Available at: https://www.theguardian.com/science/2016/jan/15/anthropomorphism-danger-humans-animals-science

Morris, S., 2022. *'Rich soup of life' in Gwent wetlands at risk from motorway*. [online] the Guardian. Available at: https://www.theguardian.com/uk-news/2018/nov/18/gwent-levels-wetlands-biodiversity-risk-wales-motorway

Nemerow, N. and Agardy, F., 1998. *Strategies of industrial and hazardous waste management*. New York: Van Nostrand Reinhold.

Nhm.ac.uk. 2022. *What is mass extinction and are we facing a sixth one?*. [online] Available at: https://www.nhm.ac.uk/discover/what-is-mass-extinction-and-are-we-facing-a-sixth-one.html

Papadaki, E. L., 2019. Feminist perspectives on objectification. *Stanford Encyclopedia of Philosophy*. Available at: https://plato.stanford.edu/entries/feminism-objectification/.

Roud, S., 2006. *The Penguin guide to the superstitions of Britain and Ireland*. London: Penguin, p.420.

Scientific American. 2022. *Wetlands Update--Has Preservation Had an Impact?*. [online] Available at: https://www.scientificamerican.com/article/wetlands-update/

Shakespeare, William., *As You Like It*, Act II, Scene I.

Shengold, L., 1991. *Soul murder: The effects of childhood abuse and deprivation*. New York: Fawcett Columbine.

Shuttle, P., 2012. *Unsent New & Selected Poems 1980-2012*. Tyne and Wear: Bloodaxe Books.

Tamás, Rebecca., 2019. *Witch*. London: Penned in the Margins.

Trickett, P.K., Noll, J.G. & Putnam, F.W., 2011. The impact of sexual abuse on female development: Lessons from a multigenerational, longitudinal research study. *Development and Psychopathology*, 23(2), pp.453–476.

Watts, J., 2019. *Concrete: The most destructive material on Earth, The Guardian*. Guardian News and Media. Available at: https://www.theguardian.com/cities/2019/feb/25/concrete-the-most-destructive-material-on-earth

Wildlifetrusts.org. 2022. *Water | The Wildlife Trusts*. [online] Available at: https://www.wildlifetrusts.org/water#

wwt.org.uk. 2022. The alternative dawn chorus: Ten quirky wetland bird calls to listen out for. [online] Available at: https://www.wwt.org.uk/news-and-stories/blog/the-alternative-dawn-chorus-ten-quirky-wetland-bird-calls-to-listen-out-for/#

Wwt.org.uk. 2022. *What is biodiversity and why do we need it?*. [online] Available at: https://www.wwt.org.uk/news-and-stories/blog/what-is-biodiversity-and-why-do-we-need-it/#

Wwt.org.uk. 2022. *Why wetlands*. [online] Available at: https://www.wwt.org.uk/our-work/why-wetlands/#

US EPA. 2022. *Why are Wetlands Important? | US EPA*. [online] Available at: https://www.epa.gov/wetlands/why-are-wetlands-important

MOON BOOKS
PAGANISM & SHAMANISM

What is Paganism? A religion, a spirituality, an alternative belief system, nature worship? You can fi nd support for all these definitions (and many more) in dictionaries, encyclopaedias, and text books of religion, but subscribe to any one and the truth will evade you. Above all Paganism is a creative pursuit, an encounter with reality, an exploration of meaning and an expression of the soul. Druids, Heathens, Wiccans and others, all contribute their insights and literary riches to the Pagan tradition. Moon Books invites you to begin or to deepen your own encounter, right here, right now.

If you have enjoyed this book, why not tell other readers by posting a review on your preferred book site.

Bestsellers from Moon Books

Keeping Her Keys
An Introduction to Hekate's Modern Witchcraft
Cyndi Brannen
Blending Hekate, witchcraft and personal development together to create a powerful new magickal perspective.
Paperback: 978-1-78904-075-3 ebook 978-1-78904-076-0

Journey to the Dark Goddess
How to Return to Your Soul
Jane Meredith
Discover the powerful secrets of the Dark Goddess and transform your depression, grief and pain into healing and integration.
Paperback: 978-1-84694-677-6 ebook: 978-1-78099-223-5

Shamanic Reiki
Expanded Ways of Working with Universal Life Force Energy
Llyn Roberts, Robert Levy
Shamanism and Reiki are each powerful ways of healing; together, their power multiplies. Shamanic Reiki introduces techniques to help healers and Reiki practitioners tap ancient healing wisdom.
Paperback: 978-1-84694-037-8 ebook: 978-1-84694-650-9

Southern Cunning
Folkloric Witchcraft in the American South
Aaron Oberon
Modern witchcraft with a Southern flair, this book is a journey through the folklore of the American South and a look at the power these stories hold for modern witches.
Paperback: 978-1-78904-196-5 ebook: 978-1-78904-197-2

For video content, author interviews and more, please subscribe to our YouTube channel.

MoonBooksPublishing

Follow us on social media for book news, promotions and more:

Facebook: Moon Books

Instagram: @MoonBooksCI

Twitter: @MoonBooksCI

TikTok: @MoonBooksCI